C

THE POCKET REFERENCE,
Second Edition

Herbert Schildt

Osborne **McGraw-Hill**

Berkeley New York St. Louis San Francisco
Auckland Bogotá Hamburg London Madrid
Mexico City Milan Montreal New Delhi Panama City
Paris São Paulo Singapore Sydney
Tokyo Toronto

Osborne **McGraw-Hill**
2600 Tenth Street
Berkeley, California 94710
U.S.A.

For information on translations or book distributors outside of the U.S.A.,
please write to Osborne **McGraw-Hill** at the above address.

C: The Pocket Reference, Second Edition

Publisher: Kenna S. Wood
Acquisitions Editor: Frances Stack
Associate Editor: Jill Pisoni
Project Editor: Judith Brown
Copy Editor: Vivian Jaquette
Proofreading Coordinator: Kelly Barr
Proofreaders: Pat Mannion, Audrey Johnson
Indexers: Phil Roberts, Peggy Bieber-Roberts
Book Designers: Erick Christgau, Peter Hancik
Typesetting: Michelle Salinaro, Peter Hancik
Cover Design: Bay Graphics Design, Inc.

34567890 DOC 99876543

ISBN 0-07-881783-8

Contents

Introduction

C was invented and first implemented by Dennis Ritchie on a DEC PDP-11 using the UNIX operating system. C is the result of a development process that started with an older language called BCPL, developed by Martin Richards. BCPL influenced a language called B, which was invented by Ken Thompson and which led to the development of C.

For many years, the de facto standard for C was the one supplied with the UNIX 5 operating system and described in *The C Programming Language* by Brian Kernighan and Dennis Ritchie (Englewood Cliffs, NJ: Prentice-Hall, 1978). It is often referred to as the "K&R standard." With the increase in popularity of microcomputers, a large number of C implementations were created. In what could almost be called a miracle, most of these implementations were highly compatible with each other on the source code level. However, because no standard existed, there were discrepancies. To alter this situation, a committee was established in the beginning of 1983 to work on the creation of an ANSI standard that would define once and for all the C language. After seven years of work, the standard was adopted in December 1989.

This pocket reference reflects the ANSI C standard. However, important aspects of the old K&R standard are also covered.

Data Types and Variables

C has a rich assortment of built-in data types available to the programmer. In addition, custom data types may be created to fit virtually any need.

The Basic Types

C has five basic built-in data types, which are listed here:

Type	C Keyword Equivalent
Character	char
Integer	int
Floating point	float
Double floating point	double
Valueless	void

The basic types (with the exception of **void**) may be modified using one or more of the following C type modifiers:

signed

unsigned

short

long

The type modifiers precede the type name that they modify.

The allowable combinations of the basic types and modifiers are shown in the following table, along with the minimal bit widths and ranges as defined by the ANSI C standard.

Type	Approximate Size in Bits	Minimal Range
char	8	−127 to 127
unsigned char	8	0 to 255
signed char	8	−127 to 127
int	16	−32767 to 32767
unsigned int	16	0 to 65535
signed int	16	Same as int
short int	16	Same as int
unsigned short int	16	0 to 65535
signed short int	16	Same as short int
long int	32	−2147483647 to 2147483647
signed long int	32	Same as long int
unsigned long int	32	0 to 4294967295
float	32	6 digits of precision
double	64	10 digits of precision
long double	128	10 digits of precision

Declaring Variables

Variable names are strings of letters or digits from one to several characters in length. (A digit cannot begin a name, however.) The maximum length of a variable name depends on your compiler. (ANSI stipulates at least 31 characters will be significant.) The underscore may also be used as part of the variable name for clarity, as in first_time. In C, uppercase and lowercase are different. For example, test and TEST are two different variables.

All variables must be declared prior to use. This is the general form of the declaration:

type variable_name;

For example, you would use the following to declare x to be a float, y to be an integer, and ch to be a character:

```
float x;
int y;
char ch;
```

You can declare more than one variable of a type by using a comma-separated list. For example, this statement declares three integers:

```
int a, b, c;
```

Initializing Variables

A variable can be initialized by following its name with an equal sign and an initial value. For example, this declaration assigns count an initial value of 100:

```
int count = 100;
```

Structures

A *structure* is a collection of variables that are grouped and referenced under one name. This is the general form of a structure declaration:

```
struct tag {
  element 1;
  element 2;

  .

  .

  .

} struct-var-list;
```

The *tag* is essentially the type name of the structure.

For example, the following structure has two elements: **name**, a character array, and **balance**, a floating-point number:

```
struct client {
  char name[80];
  float balance;
} list;
```

To reference individual structure elements, use the dot (.) operator when accessing an actual structure. The arrow operator (–>) is used when accessing the structure by using a pointer to it. For example, this statement accesses the **balance** element of **list**:

```
list.balance
```

Unions

When two or more variables share the same memory, a
union is defined. This is the general form for a **union**:

```
union tag {
   element 1;
   element 2;
     .
     .
     .
} union-var-list;
```

The *tag* is essentially the type name of the **union**.

The elements of a **union** overlay each other. For example,

```
union tom {
   char ch;
   int x;
} t;
```

declares a **union** that looks like this in memory:

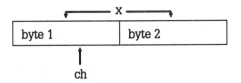

Like a structure, the individual variables that comprise the
union are referenced using the dot operator. The arrow
operator is used with a pointer to a **union**.

Enumerations

Another type of variable that can be created is called an *enumeration*. An enumeration is a list of named integer constants. As such, an enumeration type is simply a specification of the list of names that belong to the enumeration.

To create an enumeration, you must use the keyword **enum**. This is the general form of an enumeration type:

enum *tag* { *list of names* };

The *tag* is essentially the enumeration's type name. The list of named values is separated by commas.

For example, the following short program defines an enumeration of cities called **cities** and the variable **c** of type **cities**. Finally, the program will assign **c** the value "Houston".

```
enum cities {Houston, Austin, Amarillo };
enum cities c;

main(void)
{
  c = Houston;
}
```

In an enumeration, the value of the first (left-most) name is, by default, 0; the second name has the value 1, the third has the value 2, and so on. In general, each name is given a value one greater than the name it follows. You can give a name a specific value by adding an initializer. For example, in this enumeration, **Austin** will have the value 10.

```
enum cities {Houston, Austin=10, Amarillo };
```

In this example, Amarillo will have the value 11 because each name will be one greater than the one that precedes it.

The Storage Class Specifiers

The type modifiers auto, extern, register, and static are used to alter the way C creates storage for the variables that follow. These specifiers precede the type that they modify.

auto

auto tells the compiler that the local variable it precedes is created upon entry into a block and destroyed upon exit. Since all variables defined inside a function are auto by default, the auto keyword is seldom (if ever) used.

extern

If the extern modifier is placed before a variable name, the compiler will know that that variable has been declared elsewhere. The extern modifier is most commonly used when there are two or more files sharing the same global variables.

register

Traditionally, the register modifier could only be used on local integer or character variables because, according to the old Kernighan and Ritchie (K&R) standard, the register specifier causes the compiler to attempt to keep that variable in a register of the CPU instead of placing it in memory. This makes all references to that variable extremely fast. However, the ANSI C standard expanded the definition of register. It states that any variable may be specified as register and that it is the compiler's job to optimize accesses to it. For characters and integers, this still means putting them into a register in the CPU; for other types of data, it may mean using cache memory, for example. Finally, keep in mind that register is only a request. The compiler is free to ignore it. The reason for this is that only so many variables can be optimized for speed. When this limit is exceeded, the compiler will simply ignore further register requests.

Because access to register variables is very fast, they are often used to control loops, as illustrated in this example:

```
void f1(void)
{
  register int t;

  for(t=0; t<10000; ++t) {
    .
    .
    .
  }
}
```

static

The static modifier instructs the C compiler to keep a local variable in existence during the lifetime of the program instead of creating and destroying it each time it comes into and goes out of scope. Thus, making a function's local variables static allows them to maintain their values between function calls.

The static modifier may also be applied to global variables. When this is done, it causes the variable's scope to be restricted to the file in which it is declared.

Type Qualifiers

The type qualifiers **const** and **volatile** provide additional
information about the variables they precede.

const

Variables of type **const** may not be changed by your
program during execution. The compiler is free to place
variables of this type into read-only memory (ROM). For
example,

```
const int a;
```

will create an integer called **a** that may not be modified by
your program. It can, however, be used in other types of
expressions. A **const** variable will receive its value either
from an explicit initialization or by some hardware-
dependent means. The inclusion of **const** type variables
aids in the development of ROM applications.

volatile

The modifier **volatile** is used to tell the compiler that a
variable's value may be changed in ways not explicitly
specified by the program. For example, a global variable's
address may be passed to the clock routine of the
operating system and used to hold the real time of the
system. In this situation, the contents of the variable are
altered without any explicit assignment statements in the
program. This is important because some C compilers will
automatically optimize certain expressions by making the
assumption that the contents of a variable are unchanging
inside an expression in order to achieve higher
performance. The **volatile** modifier will prevent this in

those rare situations where the contents of a variable are dynamically changing.

Addressing Type Modifiers

Many C compilers designed for use with the 8086 family of processors (8086, 80186, 80286, 80386, and 80486) have added the following modifiers:

_cs, _ds, _es, _ss

far, near, huge

They may be applied to pointer declarations to allow explicit control—and override—of the default addressing mode used to compile your program.

The 8086, 80186, and 80286 use a segmented memory architecture with a total address space of one megabyte. (The 80386 and 80486 use the same scheme when operating in 8086 emulation mode.) However, this one megabyte is divided into 64K *segments*. The 8086 can directly access any byte within a segment and does so with a 16-bit register. Therefore, the address of any specific byte within the computer is the combination of the segment and the 16-bit *offset*. The segment specifies which 64K region of memory is being used, and the 16-bit offset identifies the specific byte within that segment. The segments must start on addresses that are even multiples of 16.

The 8086 uses four segment registers: one for code, one for data, one for the stack, and one extra segment. These segments are, respectively, CS, DS, SS, and ES. Each segment register is 16 bits wide.

The 8086 only loads a 16-bit address to access memory within the segment already loaded into one of its segment registers. However, if you wish to access memory outside that segment, then both the segment register and the offset must be loaded with the proper values. This effectively means that a 32-bit address is required. The difference between the two is that it takes twice as long to load two 16-bit registers as it does to load one; hence, your programs run much slower. The exact way in which a program will run slower is determined by the memory model that the program uses.

Most C compilers for the 8086 family of processors can compile your program six different ways, and each organizes the memory in the computer a little differently. The model used affects the execution speed of your program. The six models are called tiny, small, medium, compact, large, and huge. Each of these models is discussed next.

Tiny Model

The tiny model compiles a C program so that all of the segment registers are set to the same value and all addressing is done using 16 bits. This means that the code, data, and stack must all be within the same 64K segment. This method of compilation produces the smallest, fastest code. Programs compiled using this version may be converted into .COM files.

Small Model

In the small model, all addressing is done using only the 16-bit offset. The code segment is separate from the data, stack, and extra segments, which share one segment. This means that the total size of a program compiled this way is 128K, split between code and data. The addressing time is the same as that for the tiny model, but the program can be twice as big.

Medium Model

The medium model is for large programs in which the code exceeds the one-segment restriction of the small model. Here, the code may use multiple segments and requires 32-bit addresses, but the stack, data, and extra segments share one segment and use 16-bit addresses. This is good for large programs that use little data.

Compact Model

The complement of the medium model is the compact model. In this version, program code is restricted to one segment, but data may occupy several segments. This means that all accesses to data require 32-bit addressing, but the code uses 16-bit addressing. This is good for programs that require large amounts of data but little code.

Large Model

The large model allows both code and data to use multiple segments. However, the largest single item of data, such as an array, is limited to 64K. This model is used when you have both large code and large data requirements. It runs much more slowly than any of the previous versions.

Huge Model

The huge model is the same as the large model, except that individual data items may exceed 64K. This makes runtime speed degrade further.

Overriding a Memory Model

The addressing modifiers may only be applied to pointers
or to functions. When they are applied to pointers, they
affect the way data is accessed. When applied to functions,
they affect the way the function is called and returned from.

The address modifier follows the base type and precedes
the variable name. For example, the following statement
declares a **far** pointer called **f_pointer**:

```
char far *f_pointer;
```

When an address modifier is used, it causes the compiler
to use the specified addressing mode rather than the
default mode.

Arrays

You may declare arrays of any data type. This is the
general form of a singly dimensioned array:

type var-name[size];

where *size* specifies the number of elements in the array.
For example, to declare an integer array **x** of 100 elements,
you would write the following:

```
int x[100];
```

This will create an array that is 100 elements long, with the
first element being 0 and the last being 99. For example,
the following loop will load the numbers 0 through 99 into
array **x**:

```
for(t=0; t<100; t++) x[t]=t;
```

Multidimensional arrays are declared by placing the additional dimensions inside additional brackets. For example, you would write the following statement to declare a 10 by 20 integer array:

```
int x[10][20];
```

Remember, in C all array indexes begin at 0. Furthermore, C provides no array bounds-checking. Such safety checks are your responsibility.

typedef

You can create a new name for an existing type using typedef. This is its general form:

typedef *type new-name*;

For example, this statement tells the compiler that feet is another name for int:

```
typedef int feet;
```

Now, the following declaration is perfectly legal and creates an integer variable called distance:

```
feet distance;
```

Constants

In C, constants refer to fixed values that may not be altered by the program.

C constants can be of any of the basic data types. The way each constant is represented depends upon its type.

Character constants are enclosed between single quotes. For example 'a', and '%' are both character constants. Integer constants are specified as numbers without fractional components. For example, 10 and –100 are integer constants. Floating-point constants require the use of the decimal point followed by the number's fractional component. For example, 11.123 is a floating-point constant. C also allows you to use scientific notation for floating-point numbers.

There are two floating-point types: float and double. Also, there are several flavors of the basic types that are generated using the type modifiers. By default, the C compiler fits a numeric constant into the smallest compatible data type that will hold it. Therefore, 10 is an int by default, but 60000 is unsigned and 100000 is a long. Even though the value 10 could be fit into a character, the compiler will not do this because it means crossing type boundaries. The only exception to the smallest type rule is floating-point constants, which are assumed to be doubles. For virtually all programs you will write, the compiler defaults are perfectly adequate. However, it is possible to specify precisely the type of constant you want.

In cases where the default assumption that C makes about a numeric constant is not what you want, C allows you to specify the exact type of numeric constant by using a suffix. For floating-point types, if you follow the number with an F, the number is treated as a float. If you follow it with an L, the number becomes a long double. For integer types, the U suffix stands for unsigned and the L for long. Some examples are shown here:

Data Type	Constant Examples
int	1, 123, 21000, –234
long int	35000L, –34L

short int	10, −12, 90
unsigned int	10000U, 987U, 40000
float	123.23F, 4.34e−3F
double	123.23, 123123.33, −0.9876324
long double	1001.2L

Hexadecimal and Octal Constants

It is sometimes easier to use a number system based on 8 or 16 instead of 10. The number system based on 8 is called *octal* and uses the digits 0 through 7. In the octal system, the number 10 is the same as 8 in decimal. The base 16 number system is called *hexadecimal* and uses the digits 0 through 9 plus the letters A through F, which stand for 10, 11, 12, 13, 14, and 15. For example, the hexadecimal number 10 is 16 in decimal. Because of the frequency with which these two number systems are used, C allows you to specify integer constants in hexadecimal or octal instead of decimal if you prefer. A hexadecimal constant must begin with a 0x (a zero followed by an x), then specify the constant in hexadecimal form. An octal constant begins with a zero. Here are some examples:

```
int hex = 0x80;    /* 128 in decimal */
int oct = 012;     /* 10 in decimal */
```

String Constants

C supports one other type of constant in addition to those of the predefined data types: the string. A *string* is a set of characters enclosed by double quotes. For example, "this is a test" is a string. You must not confuse strings with characters. A single character constant is enclosed by single quotes, such as 'a'. However, "a" is a string containing only one letter.

Backslash Character Constants

Enclosing character constants in single quotes works for most printing characters, but a few, such as the carriage return, are impossible to enter from the keyboard. For this reason, C has created the special backslash character constants. These constants are listed here:

Code	Meaning
\b	Backspace
\f	Form feed
\n	Newline
\r	Carriage return
\t	Horizontal tab
\"	Double quote
\'	Single quote character
\0	Null
\\	Backslash
\v	Vertical tab
\a	Alert
\N	Octal constant (where N is an octal constant)
\xN	Hexadecimal constant (where N is a hexadecimal constant)

For example, the following program outputs a newline and a tab and then prints the string "This is a test".

```
#include "stdio.h"

main(void)
{
  printf("\n\tThis is a test");
}
```

Functions

A C program is a collection of one or more user-defined functions. One of the functions must be called **main** because it is at this function where execution will begin. Traditionally, **main()** is the first function in a program; however, it could go anywhere in the program.

This is the general form of a C function:

type function_name(parameter list)
{
  body of function
}

The parameter list is a comma-separated list of variables that will receive any arguments passed to the function. If the function has no parameters, then no parameter declaration is needed. For example, this function has two integer parameters called i and j, and a **double** parameter called **count**:

```
void fn1(int i, int j, double count)
{ ...
```

Notice that you must declare each parameter separately. This function declaration style reflects the function declaration approach strongly urged by the ANSI C standard. In the old K&R version of C, the function declaration would have looked like this:

```
void fn1(i, j, count)
int i, j;
double count;
{ ...
```

Remember to use the recommended ANSI standard method for new programs.

The function's return type declaration is optional—if no explicit type declaration is present, the function defaults to integer. Functions terminate and return automatically to the calling procedure when the last brace is encountered. You may force a return prior to that by using the **return** statement.

All functions (except those declared as **void**) return a value. The type of the return value must match the type declaration of the function. If no explicit type declaration has been made, then the return value is defaulted to integer. If a **return** statement is part of the function, then the return value of the function is the value in the **return** statement. If no **return** is present, then the function will return an undefined value.

Prototypes

If a function is going to return a value other than integer, then its return type must reflect this fact. Also, it will be necessary to declare the function prior to any reference to it by another piece of code. (If you don't do this, the compiler will report a "type mismatch error.") This can best be done by making a function *prototype* in the global definition area of the program. A general form of a prototype is shown here:

type name(parameter list);

In essence, a prototype is simply the return type, name, and parameter list of a function's definition, followed by a semicolon.

The example here shows how the function **fn()** is prototyped.

```c
float fn(float x); /* prototype */

main()
{
  .
  .
  .
  printf("%f", fn(0.23));
  .
  .
  .
}

float fn(float x)
{
  return x * 3.1416;
}
```

In addition to telling the compiler about the return type of a function, a function prototype also tells the compiler the number and type of the function's parameters. By using a prototype, you allow the compiler to catch mismatch errors in the types of arguments used to call a function and the types of the function's parameters.

To specify the prototype for a function that takes a variable number of arguments, use three periods at the point at which the variable number of parameters begin. For example, **printf()** could be prototyped like this:

```c
int printf(const char *format, ...);
```

The Scope and Lifetime of Variables

C has two general classes of variables: *global* and *local*. A global variable is available for use by all functions in the program, while a local variable is known and used only by the function in which it is declared. In some C literature, global variables are referred to as *external* variables and local variables are called *dynamic* or *automatic* variables. This reference uses the words *local* and *global* because they are the more commonly used terms.

A global variable must be declared outside of all functions, including the main() function. Global variables are generally placed at the top of the file, prior to main(), for ease of reading and because a variable must be declared before it is used. A local variable is declared inside a function after the function's opening brace or at the start of any block within that function. For example, the following program declares one global variable, x, and two local variables, x and y:

```c
#include "stdio.h"

int f1(void);
int x;

main(void)
{
   int y;

   y = f1();
   x = 100;
   printf("%d %d", x, x*y);
}

f1(void)
{
   int x;

   scanf("%d", &x);
   return x;
}
```

This program will multiply the number entered from the keyboard by 100. Please note that the local variable `x` in `f1()` has no relationship to the global variable `x`. This is because a local variable that has the same name as a global variable always takes precedence over the global one.

Keep in mind that local variables must be declared at the start of a function or block *before* any action statements take place.

Global variables stay in existence for the entire duration of the program, while local variables are created when the function is entered and destroyed when the function is exited. This means that local variables do not hold their values between function calls. You can use the `static` modifier, however, to preserve values between calls.

The formal parameters to a function are also local variables and, aside from their job of receiving the value of the calling arguments, behave and can be used like any other local variable.

The main() Function

All C programs must have a `main()` function. When execution begins, this is the first function called. You must not have more than one function called `main()`. When `main()` terminates, the program is over, and control passes back to the operating system.

At least two parameters are allowed to `main()`. They are `argc` and `argv`. (Some compilers will allow additional parameters.) These two variables will hold the number of command line arguments and a character pointer to them, respectively. *Command line arguments* are the information that you type in after the program name when you execute a program. For example, when you compile a C program, you type something like this:

CC MYPROG.C

where MYPROG.C is the name of the program you wish to compile and is a command line argument.

argc is an integer. Its value will always be at least 1, because the program name is the first argument as far as C is concerned. **argv** must be declared as an array of character pointers. Their usage is shown here, in a short program that will print your name on the screen.

```c
#include "stdio.h"

main(int argc, char *argv[])
{
  if(argc<2)
    printf("enter your name on the command
            line.\n");
  else
    printf("hello %s\n", argv[1]);
}
```

The C Standard Library

Unlike most other languages, C does not have built-in functions to perform disk I/O, console I/O, and a number of other useful procedures. These things are accomplished in C with the use of a set of predefined library functions that are supplied with the compiler. This library is usually called the *C standard library*. These functions are discussed later in this reference guide.

The prototypes for the functions in the library are found in *header* files, which you must include with your program. The header files that are defined by the ANSI C standard are shown in the following table.

Header File	Purpose
ASSERT.H	Defines the **assert()** macro
CTYPE.H	Character handling
ERRNO.H	Error reporting
FLOAT.H	Defines implementation-dependent floating-point values
LIMITS.H	Defines implementation-dependent various limits
LOCALE.H	Support for the **setlocale()** function
MATH.H	Various definitions used by the math library
SETJMP.H	Support for non-local jumps
SIGNAL.H	Defines signal values
STDARG.H	Support for variable-length argument lists
STDDEF.H	Defines some commonly used constants
STDIO.H	Support for file I/O
STDLIB.H	Miscellaneous declarations
STRING.H	Support for string functions
TIME.H	Support for system time functions

Operators

C has a very rich set of operators that can be divided into the following classes: arithmetic, relational and logical, bitwise, pointer, assignment, and miscellaneous.

Arithmetic Operators

C has the following seven arithmetic operators:

Operator	Action
−	Subtraction, unary minus
+	Addition
*	Multiplication
/	Division
%	Modulus division
− −	Decrement
+	Increment

The +, −, *, and / operators work in the expected fashion. The % operator returns the remainder of an integer division. The increment and decrement operators increase or decrease the operand by one.

These operators have the following order of precedence:

Precedence	Operators
Highest	++ − − −
	* / %
Lowest	+ −

Operators on the same precedence level are evaluated left to right.

Relational and Logical Operators

The relational and logical operators are used to produce
true/false results and are often used together. In C, *any*
non-zero number evaluates as true. The only value that is
false is 0. The relational and logical operators are listed in
the following tables.

Relational Operators

Operator	Meaning
>	Greater than
>=	Greater than or equal to
<	Less than
<=	Less than or equal to
==	Equal
!=	Not equal

Logical Operators

Operator	Meaning
&&	AND
||	OR
!	NOT

The relational operators are used to compare two values.
The logical operators are used to connect two values or, in
the case of NOT, to reverse a value. The precedence of
these operators is as follows:

Precedence	Operators
Highest	!
	> >= < <=
	== !=
	&&
Lowest	||

As an example, the following if statement evaluates to true and prints the line X is less than 10 :

```
X = 9;
if(X < 10) printf("X is less than 10");
```

However, in the following example, no message is displayed; both operands associated with the AND must be true for the outcome to be true.

```
X = 9;
Y = 9;
if(X < 10 && Y > 10)
   printf("X is less than 10; Y is greater");
```

The Bitwise Operators

Unlike most other programming languages, C provides operators that manipulate the actual bits inside a variable. The bitwise operators can only be used on integers or characters. They are listed here:

Operator	Meaning
&	AND
|	OR
^	XOR
~	A number's complement
>>	Right shift
<<	Left shift

AND, OR, and XOR

The truth tables for AND, OR, and XOR are shown here:

&	0	1
0	0	0
1	0	1

|	0	1
0	0	1
1	1	1

^	0	1
0	0	1
1	1	0

These rules are applied to each bit in a byte when the bitwise AND, OR, and XOR operations are performed. For example:

```
  0 1 0 0   1 1 0 1
& 0 0 1 1   1 0 1 1
- - - - - - - - - - - - - - - - - - -
  0 0 0 0   1 0 0 1


  0 1 0 0   1 1 0 1
| 0 0 1 1   1 0 1 1
- - - - - - - - - - - - - - - - - - -
  0 1 1 1   1 1 1 1


  0 1 0 0   1 1 0 1
^ 0 0 1 1   1 0 1 1
- - - - - - - - - - - - - - - - - - -
  0 1 1 1   0 1 1 0
```

In a program, you use the &, |, and ^ like any other
operators, as shown here:

```
main(void)
{
  char x, y, z;

  x = 1; y = 2; z = 4;
  x = x & y;  /* x now equals zero */

  y = x | z;  /* y now equals 4 */
}
```

The One's Complement Operator

The one's complement operator, ~, will invert all the bits in
a byte. For example, if a character variable, ch, has the bit
pattern

```
0 0 1 1   1 0 0 1
```

then

```
ch = ~ch;
```

places the bit pattern

```
1 1 0 0   0 1 1 0
```

into ch.

The Shift Operators

The right and left shift operators shift all bits—in a byte or
a word—the specified amount. As bits are shifted, zeros
are brought in. (If the value being shifted is a negative,
signed number and a right shift is performed, then 1s are
shifted in to preserve the sign.) The number on the right
side of the shift operator specifies the number of positions
to shift. These are the general forms of each shift operator:

variable >> number of bit positions

variable << number of bit positions

Given this bit pattern (and assuming an unsigned value):

```
0  0  1  1    1  1  0  1
```

a shift right yields

```
0  0  0  1  · 1  1  1  0
```

while a shift left produces

```
0  1  1  1    1  0  1  0
```

A shift right is effectively a division by 2, and a shift left is a multiplication by 2. The following code fragment will first multiply and then divide the value in x by 2.

```
int x;

x = 10;
x = x<<1;
x = x>>1;
```

Because of the way negative numbers are represented inside the machine, you must be careful if you try to use a shift for multiplication or division. Moving a 1 into the most significant bit position will make the computer think that it is a negative number.

The precedence of the bitwise operators is shown here:

Precedence	Operators
Highest	~
	>> <<
	&
	^
Lowest	|

Pointer Operators

The two pointer operators are * and &. It is unfortunate
that these operators use the same symbols as the
multiplication operator and the bitwise AND, because they
have nothing in common with them. In simple terms, a
pointer is a variable that contains the address of another
variable. Or, in different terms, the variable that contains
the address of the other is said to "point to" the other
variable.

The & Pointer Operator

The & operator returns the address of the variable it
precedes. For example, if the integer x is located at
memory address 1000, then

```
y = &x;
```

places the value 1000 into y. The & can be thought of as
"the address of." For example, the previous statement could
be read as "place the address of x into y."

The * Pointer Operator

The * is C's indirection operator. It uses the current value
of the variable it precedes as the address at which data will
be stored or obtained. For example, the following fragment:

```
y = &x; /* put address of x into y */

*y = 100; /* use address contained in y */
```

places the value 100 into x. The * can be remembered as
"at address." In this example, it could be read, "place the
value 100 at address y." Since y contains the address of x,
the value 100 is actually stored in x. In the language of C,

y is said to "point to" **x**. The * operator can also be used on the right side of an assignment. For example,

```
y = &x;

*y = 100;

z = *y/10;
```

places the value of 10 into z.

void Pointers

A pointer of type **void** is said to be a generic pointer and can be used to point to any type of object. This implies that pointers of any type can be assigned to pointers of type **void** and vice versa. To declare a **void** pointer, you will use a declaration similar to the one shown here:

```
void *p;
```

The **void** pointer is particularly useful when various types of pointers will be manipulated by a single routine.

Assignment Operators

In C, the assignment operator is the single equal sign. However, C allows a very convenient form of "shorthand" for assignments of the general type:

variable1 = variable1 operator expression;

Here are two examples:

```
x = x+10;

y = y/z;
```

Assignments of this type can be shortened to:

variable1 operator = expression;

or, specifically, in the case of the preceding examples:

```
x += 10;

y /= z;
```

The ? Operator

The **?** operator is a ternary operator that is used to replace **if** statements of the general type:

if expression1 then x = expression2

else x = expression3

The general form of the ? operator is:

variable = expression1 ? expression2 : expression3;

If *expression1* is true, then the value assigned is that of *expression2*; otherwise, it is the value of *expression3*. For example,

```
x = (y<10) ? 20 : 40;
```

will assign **x** the value of 20 if **y** is less than 10, and 40 if it is not.

The reason that this operator exists, beyond saving typing on your part, is that a C compiler can produce very fast code for this statement—much faster than for the similar **if/else** statement.

Structure and Union Operators

The . (dot) operator and the → (arrow) operator are used to reference individual elements of structures and unions. The dot operator is applied to the actual structure or union. The arrow operator is used with a pointer to a structure or a union. For example, given the structure

```
struct date_time {
  char date[16];
  int time;
} tm;
```

to assign the value "3/12/88" to element date of structure tm, you would write

```
strcpy(tm.date, "3/12/88");
```

However, assuming that p_tm is a pointer to a structure of type date_time, then the following statement is used:

```
strcpy(p_tm->date, "3/12/88");
```

The Comma Operator

The comma operator is used most often in the for statement. Its effect is to cause a sequence of operations to be performed. When it is used on the right side of an assignment statement, the value of the entire expression is the value of the last expression of the comma-separated list. For example, after execution of the following fragment:

```
y=10;

x = (y=y-5,25/y);
```

x will have the value 5 because y's original value of 10 is reduced by 5, and then that value is divided into 25,

yielding 5 as the result. You can think of the comma
operator as meaning "do this and this," and so on.

sizeof

Although sizeof is also considered a keyword, it is a
compile time operator used to determine the size, in bytes,
of a variable or data type, including user-defined structures
and unions. If used with a type, the type name must be
enclosed by parentheses.

For most microcomputer-based C compilers, this example
prints the number 2:

```
int x;

printf("%d", sizeof x);
```

The Cast

A *cast* is a special operator that forces one data type to be
converted into another. This is the general form:

(type) expression

where *type* is the desired data type.

For example, this cast causes the outcome of the specified
integer division to be of type double:

```
double d;

d = (double) 10/3;
```

Operator Precedence Summary

The table below lists the precedence of all C operators. Please note that all operators, except the unary operators and ?, associate from left to right. The unary operators, *, &, −, and ?, associate from right to left.

Precedence	Operators
Highest	() [] −> .
	! ~ ++ −− − (type) * & sizeof
	* / %
	+ −
	<< >>
	< <= > >=
	== !=
	&
	^
	|
	&&
	||
	?:
	= += −= *= /= %= >>= <<= &= ^= |=
Lowest	,

Keyword Summary

As defined by the ANSI standard, these are the 32 keywords which, combined with the formal C syntax, form the C language:

auto	double	int	struct
break	else	long	switch
case	enum	register	typedef
char	extern	return	union
const	float	short	unsigned
continue	for	signed	void
default	goto	sizeof	volatile
do	if	static	while

In addition to these, many C compilers designed for use on an 8086 family processor have added the following keywords to allow greater control over the way memory and other system resources are used:

_cs	_ss	huge	pascal
_ds	cdecl	interrupt	
_es	far	near	

All C keywords are lowercase. In C, uppercase and lowercase are different; that is, else is a keyword, but ELSE is not.

A brief description of each of the C keywords follows.

auto

auto is used to declare local variables. However, since its use is completely optional, it is seldom used.

break

break is used to exit from a do, for, or while loop, bypassing the normal loop condition. It is also used to exit from a switch statement.

An example of break in a loop is shown here:

```
while(x<100) {
  scanf("%d", &x);
  if(x < 0) break;   /* terminate if negative
                     */
  process(x);
}
```

Here, if x is negative, the loop is terminated.

A break always terminates the innermost for, do, while, or switch statement, regardless of the way these might be nested. In a switch statement, break effectively keeps program execution from "falling through" to the next case. (See "switch" for details.)

case

See "switch".

cdecl

The cdecl keyword is not part of the ANSI C standard. It forces a C compiler to compile a function so that its parameter passing conforms to the standard C calling convention. It is found in compilers that allow a Pascal calling convention to be specified. Use it when you are compiling an entire file using the Pascal option and you want a specific function to be compatible with C.

char

char is a data type used to declare character variables.

const

The const modifier tells the compiler that the variable that follows may not be modified. A const variable may, however, be given an initial value when it is declared.

continue

continue is used to bypass portions of code in a loop and force the conditional test to be performed. For example, the following while loop will simply read characters from the keyboard until an *s* is typed.

```
while(ch=getchar()) {
  if(ch != 's') continue;   /* read another
                               char */
  process(ch);
}
```

The call to **process()** will not occur until **ch** contains the character 's'.

_cs, _ds, _es, _ss

The **_cs**, **_ds**, **_es**, and **_ss** modifiers tell the C compiler which segment register to use when evaluating a pointer. These modifiers are not defined by the ANSI C standard and apply only to compilers designed for the 8086 family of processors.

For example, this fragment instructs the compiler to use the extra segment when using **ptr**:

```
int _es *ptr;
```

There probably will be few, if any, times that you will need to use these segment register overrides.

default

default is used in the **switch** statement to signal a default block of code to be executed if no matches are found in the **switch**. (See "**switch**".)

do

The **do** loop is one of three loop constructs available in C. This is the general form of the **do** loop:

```
do {
    statement block
} while(condition);
```

If only one statement is repeated, the braces are not necessary, but they do add clarity to the statement.

The **do** loop is the only loop in C that will always have at least one iteration, because the condition is tested at the bottom of the loop.

A common use of the **do** loop is for reading disk files. The fragment shown here will read a file until an EOF is encountered.

```
do {
    ch = getc(fp);
    store(ch);
} while(!feof(fp));
```

double

double is a data type specifier used to declare double-precision floating-point variables.

else

See "**if**".

enum

The enum type specifier is used to create enumeration types. An enumeration is simply a list of named integer constants. Hence, an enumeration type specifies what that list comprises. The general form of an enumeration is shown here:

enum tag {name list} var-list;

The *tag* is essentially the type name of the enumeration. The *var-list* is optional and enumeration variables may be declared separately from the type definition, as the following example shows. This code declares an enumeration called color and a variable of that type called c, and performs an assignment and a conditional test:

```
enum color {red, green, yellow};
enum color c;

main(void)
{
  c = red;
  if(c==red) printf("is red\n");
}
```

For more information on enumerations, refer to the section, "Data Types and Variables," of this book.

extern

extern is a data type modifier used to tell the compiler that a variable is declared elsewhere in the program. This is often used in conjunction with separately compiled files that share the same global data and are linked together. In essence, it notifies the compiler about the type of a variable without redeclaring it.

As an example, if first were declared in another file as an integer, then the following declaration would be used in subsequent files.

```
extern int first;
```

far

The far type modifier is not part of the ANSI C standard. It is used by compilers designed for use on the 8086 family of processors. far forces a pointer variable to use 32- rather than 16-bit addressing.

float

float is a data type specifier used to declare floating-point variables.

for

The for loop allows automatic initialization and incrementation of a counter variable. This is the general form:

```
for(initialization; condition; increment) {
    statement block
}
```

If the *statement block* is only one statement, the braces are not necessary.

Although the `for` allows a number of variations, generally the *initialization* is used to set a counter variable to its starting value. The *condition* is generally a relational statement that checks the counter variable against a termination value, and *increment* increments (or decrements) the counter variable.

It is important to understand that, if the *condition* is false to begin with, the body of the `for` will not execute even once.

The following code will print the message "hello" 10 times.

```
for(t=0; t<10; t++) printf("hello\n");
```

goto

The `goto` keyword causes program execution to "jump" to the label specified in the `goto` statement. Here is the general form of `goto`:

```
goto label;

    .

    .

    .

label:
```

All labels must end in a colon, and they must not conflict with keywords or function names. Furthermore, a `goto` can only branch within the current function—not from one function to another.

The following example will print the message "right" but not the message "wrong".

```
goto lab1;
  printf("wrong");
lab1:
  printf("right");
```

huge

The huge type modifier is not part of the ANSI standard. It is used by compilers designed for use on the 8086 family of processors to force a pointer variable to use 32- rather than 16-bit addressing. It also allows the object pointed to by a huge pointer to be larger than one segment (64K).

if

This is the general form of the if statement:

```
if(condition) {
  statement block 1
}
else {
  statement block 2
}
```

If single statements are used, the braces are not needed. The else is optional.

The condition may be any expression. If that expression evaluates to any value other than 0, then *statement block 1* will be executed; otherwise, if it exists, *statement block 2* will be executed.

The following fragment checks for the letter *q*, which terminates the program.

```
ch = getchar();
if(ch == 'q') {
  printf("program terminated");
  exit(0);
}
else proceed();
```

int

int is the type specifier used to declare integer variables.

interrupt

The interrupt type specifier is not part of the ANSI standard. It is used to declare functions that will be used as interrupt service routines.

long

long is a data type modifier used to declare double-length integer variables.

near

The near type modifier is not part of the ANSI standard. It is used by compilers designed for use on the 8086 family of processors to force a pointer variable to use 16- rather than 32-bit addressing.

pascal

The pascal keyword is not defined by the ANSI C standard. It is used to force a C compiler to compile a function in such a way that its parameter passing convention is compatible with Pascal rather than C.

register

register is a storage class modifier used to request that access to a variable be optimized for speed. Traditionally, register could be used only on integer or character variables; it causes these variables to be stored in a register of the CPU instead of being placed in memory. The ANSI C standard broadened its definition to include all types of data. However, data other than integers and characters cannot usually be stored in a CPU register. For other types of data, either cache memory (or some other sort of optimizing scheme) is used or the register request is ignored.

register can only be used on local variables. See the section, "Data Types and Variables," of this book for more details.

return

The return statement forces a return from a function and can be used to transfer a value back to the calling routine.

For example, the following function returns the product of its two integer arguments.

```
mul(int a, int b)
{
  return(a*b);
}
```

Keep in mind that as soon as a return is encountered, the function will return, skipping any other code that may be in the function.

Remember also that a function can contain more than one return statement.

short

short is a data type modifier used to declare short integers.

signed

The signed type modifier is used to specify a signed char data type.

sizeof

The sizeof compile time operator returns the length of the variable or type it precedes. If it precedes a type, then that type must be enclosed in parentheses. If it precedes a variable, the parentheses are optional. For example, given the following:

```
int i;
printf("%d", sizeof(int));
printf("%d", sizeof i);
```

both printf() statements will print 2 for most PC-based C compilers.

sizeof's principal use is to help generate portable code when that code depends upon the size of the C built-in data types.

static

static is a data type modifier used to instruct the compiler to create permanent storage for the local variable that it precedes. This enables the specified variable to maintain its value between function calls.

struct

The struct keyword is used to create complex or conglomerate variables, called *structures*, that are made up of one or more elements. This is the general form of a structure:

```
struct tag {
    type element1;
    type element2;

      .

      .

      .
    type elementn;
} struct-var-list;
```

The *tag* is essentially the type name of the structure. The individual elements are referenced by using the dot when operating on a structure or by using the arrow operator when operating through a pointer to the structure.

For example, the following structure contains a string called **name** and two integers called **high** and **low**. It also declares one variable called **my_var**.

```
struct my_struct {
  char name[80];
  int high;
  int low;
} my_var;
```

The section, "Data Types and Variables," of this book covers this in more detail.

switch

The **switch** statement is C's multi-way branch statement. It is used to route execution one of several different ways. This is the general form of the **switch** statement:

```
switch (control_var) {
  case constant 1: statement sequence 1;
    break
  case constant 2: statement sequence 2;
    break;

    .

    .

    .

  case constant n: statement sequence n;
    break;
  default: default statements;
}
```

Each statement sequence may be from one to several statements long. The **default** portion is optional.

switch works by checking the *control_var* against the constants. If a match is found, that sequence of statements is executed. If the statement sequence associated with the case that matches the value of *control_var* does not contain a break, execution will continue on into the next case. Put differently, from the point of the match, execution will continue until either a break statement is found or the switch ends. If no match is found and a default case exists, its statement sequence is executed. Otherwise, no action takes place. The following example processes a menu selection.

```
ch = getchar();

switch (ch) {
  case 'e': enter();
      break;
  case 'l': list();
      break;
  case 's': sort();
      break;
  case 'q': exit(0);
  default: printf("unknown command\n");
      printf("try again\n");

}
```

typedef

The typedef keyword allows you to create a new name for an existing data type. The data type may be either one of the built-in types, or a structure, union, or enumeration. Here is the general form of typedef:

```
typedef type_specifier new_name;
```

For example, to use the word balance in place of float, you would write the following:

```
typedef float balance;
```

union

union is used to assign two or more variables to the same memory location. The form of the definition and the way the . (dot) and –> (arrow) operators reference an element are the same as for struct. This is the general form:

```
union tag {
  type element 1;
  type element 2;

    .

    .

    .

  type element n;
} union-var-list;
```

The *tag* is essentially the type name for the union. For example, this creates a union between a double and a character string and creates one variable called my_var:

```
union my_union {
  char time[30];
  double offset;
} my_var;
```

This is covered in more detail in the section, "Data Types and Variables," of this book.

unsigned

unsigned is a data type modifier that tells the compiler to eliminate the sign bit of an integer and to use all bits for arithmetic. This has the effect of doubling the size of the largest integer, but restricts it to only positive numbers.

void

The `void` type specifier is primarily used to explicitly declare functions that return no (meaningful) value. It is also used to create `void` pointers (pointers to `void`), which are generic pointers capable of pointing to any type of object.

volatile

The `volatile` modifier is used to tell the compiler that a variable may have its contents altered in ways not explicitly defined by the program. For example, variables that are changed by hardware such as realtime clocks, interrupts, or other inputs should be declared as `volatile`.

while

The `while` loop has the following general form:

```
while(condition) {
    statement block
}
```

If a single statement is the object of the `while`, then the braces may be omitted.

while tests its *condition* at the top of the loop. Therefore, if the *condition* is false to begin with, the loop will not execute even once. The *condition* may be any expression.

An example of a **while** loop is shown here. It will read 100 characters from a disk file and store them into a character array.

```
char s[256];

t = 0;

while(t<100) {
  s[t] = getc(fp);
  t++;
}
```

The C Preprocessor

C includes several preprocessor directives that are used to give instructions to the compiler. The preprocessor directives are listed here:

#define

#elif

#else

#endif

#error

#if

#ifdef

#ifndef

#include

#line

#pragma

#undef

These are each discussed briefly in this section. (The related directives, #elif, #else, #endif, #ifdef, and #ifndef are all discussed under #if.)

#define

#define is used to perform macro-substitutions of one piece of text for another throughout the file in which it is used. This is the general form of the directive:

#define *name character-sequence*

Notice that there is no semicolon in this statement. Furthermore, once the character sequence has started, it is terminated only by the end of the line.

For example, if you wish to use the word TRUE for the value 1 and the word FALSE for the value 0, then declare these two macro #defines:

```
#define TRUE 1
#define FALSE 0
```

This will cause the compiler to substitute a 1 or a 0 each time the name TRUE or FALSE is encountered.

The #define directive has another powerful feature: The macro can have arguments. A macro that takes arguments acts much like a function. Each time the macro is encountered, the arguments associated with it are replaced by the actual arguments found in the program. For example,

```
#include "stdio.h"

#define ABS(a)  (a)<0 ? -(a) : (a)

main(void)
{
  printf("abs of -1 and 1: %d %d", ABS(-1),
          ABS(1));

  return 0;
}
```

When this program is compiled, a in the macro definition
will be substituted with the values –1 and 1. The
parentheses surrounding a are necessary to ensure proper
substitution in all cases. For example, if the parentheses
around a were removed, this expression:

```
ABS(10-20)
```

would be converted to

```
10-20<0 ? -10-20 : 10-20
```

thus yielding the wrong result.

The use of macro-substitutions in place of real functions
has one major benefit: it increases the speed of the code
because no overhead for a function call is incurred.
However, this increased speed is paid for with a possible
increase in the size of the program because of duplicated
code.

#error

The **#error** directive forces the compiler to stop
compilation when it is encountered. It is used primarily for
debugging. Here is its general form:

#error *message*

When **#error** is encountered, the message and the line
number are displayed.

#if, #ifdef, #ifndef, #else, #elif, #endif

These preprocessor directives are used to selectively compile various portions of a program. The general idea is that if the expression after an #if, #ifdef, or #ifndef is true, then the code that is between one of the preceding and an #endif will be compiled; otherwise, it will be skipped over. #endif is used to mark the end of an #if block. The #else directive can be used with any of the above in a manner similar to the else in the C if statement.

This is the general form of #if:

#if constant-expression

If the constant expression is true, then the block of code will be compiled.

This is the general form of #ifdef:

#ifdef macro-name

If the macro-name has been defined in a #define statement, then the following block of code will be compiled.

This is the general form of #ifndef:

#ifndef macro-name

If macro-name is currently undefined by a #define statement, then the block of code is compiled.

For example, here is the way some of the preprocessor directives work together. The following code:

```
#include "stdio.h"

#define ted 10

main(void)
{
#ifdef ted
  printf("Hi Ted\n");
#endif
  printf("bye bye\n");
#if 10<9
  printf("Hi George\n");
#endif
}
```

will print "Hi Ted" and "bye bye" on the screen, but not "Hi George".

The #elif directive is used to create an if-else-if statement. Here is its general form:

#elif *constant-expression*

#elif may be used with #if but not with #ifdef or #ifndef.

You can also use #if or #elif to determine if a macro name is defined using the defined preprocessing operator. It takes this general form:

#if defined *macro-name*

   statement sequence

#endif

If the *macro-name* is defined, then the statement sequence will be compiled; otherwise, it will be skipped. For

example, this program compiles the conditional code
because DEBUG is defined by the program:

```
#include "stdio.h"

#define DEBUG

main()
{
  int i=100;
/* ... */
#if defined DEBUG
  printf("value of i is: %d\n", i);
#endif
/*...*/
}
```

You can also precede defined with the ! operator to cause
conditional compilation when the macro is not defined.

#include

The #include preprocessor directive instructs the compiler
to read and compile another source file. It takes these
general forms:

#include "filename"

#include <filename>

The source file to be read in must be enclosed between
double quotes or angle brackets. If the filename is enclosed
by angle brackets, the file is searched for in a manner
defined by the creator of the compiler. Often, this means
searching some special directory set aside for include files.
If the filename is enclosed in quotes, the file is looked for in

another implementation-defined manner. For many implementations, this means searching the current working directory. If the file is not found, then the search is repeated as if the filename had been enclosed in angle brackets. You must check your compiler's user manual for details on the differences between angle brackets and double quotes.

#includes may be nested within other included files.

For example,

```
#include "stdio.h"
```

will instruct the C compiler to read and compile the header for the disk file library routines.

#line

The #line directive is used to change the contents of _ _LINE_ _ and _ _FILE_ _, which are predefined identifiers in the compiler. This is the basic form of the command:

```
#line number "filename"
```

where number is any positive integer and filename is any valid file identifier. The number becomes the number of the current source line and the filename becomes the name of the source file. The name of the file is optional. #line is primarily used for debugging purposes and special applications.

The _ _LINE_ _ identifier is an integer, and _ _FILE_ _ is a null-terminated string.

For example, the following sets the current line counter to 10 and the file to "test":

```
#line 10 "test"
```

#pragma

The #pragma directive is an implementation-defined directive that allows various instructions to be given to the compiler. For example, a compiler may have an option to support the tracing of program execution. A trace option would then be specified by a #pragma statement. You must check the user manual of the compiler for details and options.

#undef

The #undef directive is used to remove a previously defined definition of the macro-name that follows it. This is the general form:

```
#undef macro-name
```

For example, in the following code,

```
#define LEN 100
#define WIDTH 100

char array[LEN][WIDTH];

#undef LEN
#undef WIDTH
/* at this point both LEN and WIDTH are
   undefined */
```

both LEN and WIDTH are defined until the #undef
statements are encountered.

The principal use of #undef is to allow macro-names to be
localized to only those sections of code that need them.

The # and ## Preprocessor Operators

ANSI C provides two preprocessor operators: # and ##.
These operators are used in a macro #define.

The # operator causes the argument it precedes to be
turned into a quoted string. For example, consider this
program:

```c
#include "stdio.h"

#define mkstr(s)   # s

main(void)
{
  printf(mkstr(I like C++));

  return 0;
}
```

The C preprocessor turns the line

```c
printf(mkstr(I like C));
```

into

```c
printf("I like C");
```

The ## operator is used to concatenate two tokens. For example, in the following program,

```c
#include "stdio.h"

#define concat(a, b)   a ## b

main(void)
{
  int xy = 10;

  printf("%d", concat(x, y));

  return 0;
}
```

the preprocessor transforms

```c
printf("%d", concat(x, y));
```

into

```c
printf("%d", xy);
```

If these operators seem strange to you, keep in mind that they are not needed or used in most C programs. They exist primarily to allow some special cases to be handled by the preprocessor.

Predefined Macro Names

The ANSI C standard specifies five built-in predefined macro names. They are

_ _LINE_ _

_ _FILE_ _

_ _DATE_ _

_ _TIME_ _

_ _STDC_ _

If your compiler is non-standard, then some or all of these may be missing. Remember also that your compiler may supply more predefined macros for your use.

The _ _LINE_ _ and _ _FILE_ _ macros are discussed under "#line". The others will be examined here.

The _ _DATE_ _ macro is a string in the form month/day/year that is the date of the translation of the source file into object code.

The time of the translation of the source code into object code is contained as a string in _ _TIME_ _. The form of the string is hour:minute:second.

The macro _ _STDC_ _ contains the decimal constant 1. This means that the implementation is a standard-conforming implementation. If it is any other number, then the implementation must vary from the standard.

I/O Functions

The functions that comprise the C input/output system can be grouped into three major categories: the ANSI C standard I/O, UNIX-like I/O, and direct (or hardware-specific) I/O. This section describes all three, with more emphasis on the ANSI I/O system.

The header file associated with the ANSI standard I/O functions is called STDIO.H. It defines several macros and types used by the file system. The most important type is FILE, which is used to declare a file pointer. Two other types are size_t and fpos_t, which are essentially equivalent to unsigned. The size_t type defines an object that is capable of holding the size of the largest file allowed by the operating environment. The fpos_t type defines an object that can hold all of the information needed to uniquely specify every position within a file.

The ANSI file system operates through streams. A *stream* is a logical device that is connected to an actual physical device, which is referred to as the *file*, when a file is opened. In the ANSI I/O system, all streams have the same capabilities, but files may have differing qualities. For example, a disk file allows random access, but a modem does not. Thus, the ANSI C I/O system provides a level of abstraction between the programmer and the physical device. The abstraction is the stream and the device is the file. In this way, a consistent logical interface can be maintained even though the actual physical devices may differ.

A stream is connected to a file via a call to fopen(). Streams are operated upon through the *file pointer*, which is a pointer of type FILE *. In a sense, the file pointer is the glue that holds the ANSI C I/O system together.

When your program begins execution, three predefined streams are automatically opened. They are **stdin**, **stdout**, and **stderr**, which refer to standard input, standard output, and standard error, respectively. By default, these are connected to the console, but they may be redirected to any other type of device.

Many of the functions defined by ANSI set the built-in global integer variable **errno** when an error occurs. Your program can check this variable when an error occurs to obtain more information about the error. The values that **errno** may take are implementation dependent.

The UNIX-like I/O system is not defined by the ANSI C standard and is expected to decline in popularity. The most commonly used UNIX-like I/O system functions are included in this chapter because they are still widely used in existing programs. For many C compilers, the header file related to the UNIX-like file system is called IO.H. Your system may be different; check your user manual for details.

Unlike the ANSI C I/O system that works through streams, the UNIX-like I/O system uses *file descriptors*, which are integers. In the UNIX-like file system, each file is associated with a unique file descriptor, which is obtained through a call to **open()** or **creat()**.

For DOS-based compilers, the direct I/O functions generally use the CONIO.H header file. (Be sure to check your user manual, however, because this file might be called something else.) I/O functions are defined by the ANSI C standard.

Also included in this chapter are some functions that are not defined by either the ANSI C or UNIX standard. They are included because they are common extensions found in many different implementations.

cgets

```
#include "conio.h"
char *cgets(char *str);
```

The cgets() function is not defined by the ANSI C
standard. It is commonly included in the library of
DOS-based compilers.

The cgets() function reads a string entered from the
keyboard into the array pointed to by *str*. Prior to the call to
cgets(), the first byte of *str* must be set to the maximum
length of the string you want to read. Upon return, the
second byte of *str* will contain the number of characters
actually read. Therefore, the array pointed to by *str* must be
at least two bytes longer than the largest string you want
to read. After inputting the string, the user enters a
carriage return, which is converted into a null to terminate
the string.

The cgets() function returns a pointer to *str[2]*.

In some implementations, cgets() does not allow
redirection to devices other than the keyboard. Also,
cgets() may operate relative to a window rather than the
screen. Check your user manual for details.

Related functions are cputs(), gets(), fgets(), and puts().

clearerr

```
#include "stdio.h"
void clearerr(FILE *stream);
```

The clearerr() function takes the file error flag pointed to by *stream* and resets it to zero (off). The end-of-file indicator is also reset.

The error flags for each stream are initially set to zero by a successful call to fopen(). Once an error has occurred, the flags stay set until an explicit call to either clearerr() or rewind() is made.

File errors can occur for a wide variety of reasons, many of which are system dependent. The exact nature of the error can be determined by calling perror(), which displays the reason that the error occurred (see perror()).

Related functions are feof(), ferror(), and perror().

close

```
#include "io.h"
int close(int fd);
```

The close() function belongs to the UNIX-like file system and is not defined by the ANSI C standard. When close() is called with a valid file descriptor, it closes the file associated with it and flushes the write-buffers (if applicable). (File descriptors are created through a successful call to open() or creat() and do not relate to streams or file pointers.)

When successful, close() returns 0; otherwise, −1 is returned. Although there are several reasons that a file may not be able to be closed, the most common is the premature removal of the medium. For example, if a diskette is removed from the drive before the file is closed, an error will result when there is a call to close().

Related functions are open(), creat(), read(), write(), and unlink().

cprintf

```
#include "conio.h"
int cprintf(const char *format, ...);
```

The cprintf() function is not defined by the ANSI C standard. It is commonly included in the library of DOS-based compilers.

The cprintf() function operates exactly like printf() except that, in many implementations, its output is not redirectable to other devices. Also, in some environments, cprintf() operates relative to a window instead of the screen. Check your user manual for details.

Related functions are cscanf() and cputs().

cputs

```
#include "conio.h"
int cputs(const char *str);
```

The cputs() function is not defined by the ANSI C standard. It is commonly included in the library of DOS-based compilers.

The cputs() function outputs the string pointed to by *str* to the screen. In some implementations, its output may not be redirected. Also, for some environments, cputs() may output its string relative to a window rather than the screen. Refer to your user manual for details.

cputs() returns the last character written if successful and **EOF** on failure.

A related function is **cprintf()**.

creat

```
#include "io.h"
int creat(char *filename, int pmode);
```

The **creat()** function is part of the UNIX-like file system and is not defined by the ANSI C standard. Its purpose is to create a new file with the name pointed to by *filename* and to open it for writing. If successful, **creat()** returns a file descriptor that is greater than or equal to 0; on failure, –1 is returned. (File descriptors are integers and do not relate to streams or file pointers.)

The value of *pmode* determines the file's access setting, sometimes called its *permission mode*. The value of *pmode* is highly dependent upon the operating system; you must check the user manual for exact details. In general, the access modes that a file may have include read-only, read/write, and a security-access setting. For many compilers, the values of *pmode* are defined as macros in the header file called STAT.H (which is sometimes found in the SYS directory). The commonly used macro names and their meanings are shown here.

S_IWRITE	Allow output
S_IREAD	Allow input
S_IREAD | S_IWRITE	Allow input/output

If, at the time of the call to creat(), the specified file is already existent, it will be erased. All previous contents will be lost.

Related functions are open(), close(), read(), write(), unlink(), and eof().

cscanf

```
#include "conio.h"
int cscanf(const char *format, ...);
```

The cscanf() function is not defined by the ANSI C standard. It is commonly included in the library of DOS-based compilers.

The cscanf() function operates exactly like scanf() except that, in many implementations, its input cannot be redirected to any device other than the keyboard. Also, in some environments, cscanf() operates relative to a window instead of the screen. Check your user manual for details.

Related functions are cprintf() and cgets().

eof

```
#include "io.h"
int eof(int fd);
```

The eof() function is part of the UNIX-like file system and is not defined by the ANSI standard. When called with a valid file descriptor, eof() returns 1 if the end of the file has been reached; otherwise, 0 is returned. If an error has occurred, −1 is returned.

Related functions are open(), close(), read(), write(), and unlink().

fclose

```
#include "stdio.h"
int fclose(FILE *stream);
```

The fclose() function closes the file associated with *stream* and flushes its buffer. After an fclose(), *stream* is no longer connected with the file, and any automatically allocated buffers are deallocated.

If fclose() is successful, 0 is returned; otherwise, a non-zero value is returned. Trying to close a file that has already been closed will result in an error. Removing the storage media before closing a file will also generate an error, as will lack of sufficient free disk space.

Related functions are fopen(), freopen(), and fflush().

feof

```
#include "stdio.h"
int feof(FILE *stream);
```

The feof() function checks the file position indicator to determine whether the end of the file associated with *stream* has been reached. A non-zero value is returned if the file position indicator is at end-of-file; 0 is returned otherwise.

Once the end of the file has been reached, subsequent read operations will return EOF until either rewind() is called or the file position indicator is moved using fseek(). The macro EOF is defined in STDIO.H.

The feof() function is particularly useful when working with binary files because the end-of-file marker is also a valid binary integer. Explicit calls must be made to feof(); you cannot simply test the return value of getc(), for example, to determine when the end of a binary file has been reached.

Related functions are clearerr(), ferror(), perror(), putc(), and getc().

ferror

```
#include "stdio.h"
int ferror(FILE *stream);
```

The ferror() function checks for a file error on the given *stream*. A return value of 0 indicates that no error has occurred, while a non-zero value indicates an error.

The error flags associated with *stream* will stay set until either the file is closed or rewind() or clearerr() is called.

To determine the exact nature of the error, use the perror() function.

Related functions are clearerr(), feof(), and perror().

fflush

```
#include "stdio.h"
int fflush(FILE *stream);
```

If *stream* is associated with a file opened for writing, a call to fflush() causes the contents of the output buffer to be physically written to the file. If *stream* points to an input file, then the contents of the input buffer are cleared. In either case, the file remains open.

A return value of 0 indicates success; EOF is returned if a write error has occurred.

All buffers are automatically flushed upon normal termination of the program or when they are full. Closing a file also flushes its buffer.

Related functions are fclose(), fopen(), fread(), fwrite(), getc(), and putc().

fgetc

```
#include "stdio.h"
int fgetc(FILE *stream);
```

The fgetc() function returns the next character from the input *stream* from the current position and increments the file position indicator. The character is read as an unsigned char that is converted to an integer.

If the end of the file is reached, fgetc() returns EOF. However, since EOF is a valid integer value, when working with binary files, you must use feof() to check for end-of-file. EOF is also returned if fgetc() encounters an error. Again, if working with binary files, you must use ferror() to check for file errors.

Related functions are fputc(), getc(), putc(), and fopen().

fgetpos

```
#include "stdio.h"
int fgetpos(FILE *stream, fpos_t *position);
```

The fgetpos() function stores the current value of the file
position indicator in the object pointed to by *position*. The
object pointed to by *position* must be of type fpos_t,
which is a type defined in STDIO.H. The value stored there
is useful only in a subsequent call to fsetpos().

If an error occurs, fgetpos() returns non-zero; otherwise, it
returns 0.

Related functions are fsetpos(), fseek(), and ftell().

fgets

```
#include "stdio.h"
char *fgets(char *str, int num, FILE
            *stream);
```

The fgets() function reads up to *num–1* characters from
stream and places them into the character array pointed to
by *str*. Characters are read until either a newline character
or an EOF is received, or until the specified limit is
reached. After the characters have been read, a null is
placed in the array immediately after the last character
read. A newline character will be retained and will be part
of *str*.

If successful, fgets() returns *str*; a null pointer is returned
upon failure. If a read error occurs, the contents of the array
pointed to by *str* are indeterminate. Because a null pointer
will be returned when either an error has occurred or when

the end of the file is reached, you should use feof() or ferror() to determine what has actually happened.

Related functions are fputs(), fgetc(), gets(), and puts().

fopen

```
#include "stdio.h"
FILE *fopen(const char *fname, const char
            *mode);
```

The fopen() function opens the file whose name is pointed to by *fname* and returns the stream that is associated with it. The operations that will be allowed on the file are defined by the value of *mode*. The legal values for *mode*, as specified by the ANSI C standard, are shown in the following table. The filename must be a string of characters that comprise a valid filename as defined by the operating system and may include a path specification if the environment supports it.

Mode	Meaning
"r"	Open text file for reading
"w"	Create a text file for writing
"a"	Append to text file
"rb"	Open binary file for reading
"wb"	Create binary file for writing
"ab"	Append to a binary file
"r+"	Open text file for read/write
"w+"	Create text file for read/write
"a+"	Open text file for read/write
"rb+"	Open binary file for read/write

Mode	Meaning
"wb+"	Create binary file for read/write
"ab+"	Open binary file for read/write

If fopen() is successful in opening the specified file, then a FILE pointer is returned. If the file cannot be opened, a null pointer is returned.

As the table shows, a file may be opened in either text or binary mode. In text mode, some character translations may occur. For example, newline characters may be converted into carriage return/linefeed sequences. No such translations occur on binary files.

The correct method of opening a file is illustrated by this code fragment.

```
FILE *fp;

if ((fp = fopen("test", "w"))==NULL) {
  puts("cannot open file\n");
  exit(1);
}
```

This method detects any error in opening a file, such as a write-protected file or a full disk, before attempting to write to it. A null is used to indicate an error because no file pointer will ever have that value. NULL is defined in STDIO.H.

If you use fopen() to open a file for output, then any pre-existing file by that name will be erased and a new file started. If no file by that name exists, then one will be created.

If you want to add to the end of the file, then you must use mode "a". If the file does not exist, an error will be returned. Opening a file for read operations requires that the file exist. If it does not exist, an error will be returned. Finally, if a file is opened for read/write operations, it will not be erased if it exists; however, if it does not exist, it will be created.

When accessing a file opened for read/write operations, you may not follow an output operation with an input operation (or follow an input operation with an output operation) without first making an intervening call to either fflush(), fseek(), fsetpos(), or rewind().

Related functions are fclose(), fread(), fwrite(), putc(), and getc().

fprintf

```
#include "stdio.h"
int fprintf(FILE *stream, const char
            *format, ...);
```

The fprintf() function outputs the values of the arguments that comprise the argument list, as specified in the *format* string, to the stream pointed to by *stream*. The return value is the number of characters actually printed. If an error occurs, a negative number is returned.

There may be from zero to several arguments, with the maximum number being system dependent.

The operations of the format control string and commands are identical to those in printf(); see the section on the printf() function for a complete description.

Related functions are printf() and fscanf().

fputc

```
#include "stdio.h"
int fputc(int ch, FILE *stream);
```

The fputc() function writes the character *ch* to the specified stream at the current file position and then advances the file position indicator. Even though *ch* is declared to be an int for historical purposes, it is converted by fputc() into an unsigned char. Because all character arguments are elevated to integers at the time of the call, you will generally see character variables used as arguments. If an integer were used, the high-order byte would simply be discarded.

The value returned by fputc() is the value of the character written. If an error occurs, EOF is returned. For files opened for binary operations, an EOF may be a valid character; the function ferror() will need to be used to determine whether an error has actually occurred.

Related functions are fgetc(), fopen(), fprintf(), fread(), and fwrite().

fputchar

```
#include "stdio.h"
int fputchar(int ch);
```

The fputchar() function writes the character *ch* to stdout. This function is not defined by the ANSI C standard, but is a common addition. Even though *ch* is declared to be an int for historical purposes, it is converted by fputchar() into an unsigned char. Because all character arguments are elevated to integers at the time of the call, you will generally see character variables used as arguments. If an integer were used, the high-order byte would simply be discarded. A call to fputchar() is the functional equivalent of a call to fputc(ch, stdout).

The value returned by fputchar() is the value of the character written. If an error occurs, EOF is returned. For files opened for binary operations, a EOF may be a valid character; the function ferror() will need to be used to determine whether an error has actually occurred.

Related functions are fgetc(), fopen(), fprintf(), fread(), and fwrite().

fputs

```
#include "stdio.h"
int fputs(const char *str, FILE *stream);
```

The fputs() function writes the contents of the string pointed to by *str* to the specified stream. The null terminator is not written.

The fputs() function returns a non-negative value on success and EOF on failure.

If the stream is opened in text mode, certain character translations may take place. This means that there may not be a one-to-one mapping of the string onto the file. However, if the stream is opened in binary mode, no character translations will occur, and a one-to-one mapping between the string and the file will exist.

Related functions are fgets(), gets(), puts(), fprintf(), and fscanf().

fread

```
#include "stdio.h"
int fread(void *buf, size_t size, size_t
          count, FILE *stream);
```

The fread() function reads *count* number of objects, each object being *size* bytes in length, from the stream pointed to by *stream*, and places them in the array pointed to by *buf*. The file position indicator is advanced by the number of characters read.

The fread() function returns the number of items actually read. If less items are read than are requested in the call, either an error has occurred or the end of the file has been reached. You must use feof() or ferror() to determine what has taken place.

If the stream is opened for text operations, then certain character translations, such as carriage-return/linefeed sequences being transformed into newline characters, may occur.

Related functions are fwrite(), fopen(), fscanf(), fgetc(), and getc().

freopen

```
#include "stdio.h"
FILE *freopen(const char *fname, const char
              *mode, FILE *stream);
```

The freopen() function associates an existing stream with a different file. The new file's name is pointed to by *fname*, the access mode is pointed to by *mode*, and the stream to be reassigned is pointed to by *stream*. The *mode* string uses the same format as it does for fopen(); a complete discussion is found in the fopen() section.

When called, freopen() first tries to close a file that may currently be associated with *stream*. However, if the attempt to close the file fails, the freopen() function still opens the other file.

The freopen() function returns a pointer to *stream* on success and a null pointer otherwise.

The main use of freopen() is to redirect the system-defined streams stdin, stdout, and stderr to some other file.

Related functions are fopen() and fclose().

fscanf

```
#include "stdio.h"
int fscanf(FILE *stream, const char *format,
           ...);
```

The fscanf() function works exactly like the scanf() function except that it reads the information from the stream specified by *stream* instead of stdin. See the description of the scanf() function for details.

The fscanf() function returns the number of arguments actually assigned values. This number does not include skipped fields. A return value of EOF means that a failure occurred before the first assignment was made.

Related functions are scanf() and fprintf().

fseek

```
#include "stdio.h"
int fseek(FILE *stream, long offset, int
          origin);
```

The fseek() function sets the file position indicator
associated with *stream* according to the values of *offset*
and *origin*. Its purpose is to support random I/O operations.
The *offset* is the number of bytes from *origin* to seek to.
The values for *origin* must be one of these macros (defined
in STDIO.H).

Name	Meaning
SEEK_SET	Seek from start of file
SEEK_CUR	Seek from current location
SEEK_END	Seek from end of file

A return value of 0 means that fseek() succeeded. A
non-zero value indicates failure.

You may use fseek() to move the position indicator
anywhere in the file, even beyond the end. However, it is
an error to attempt to set the position indicator before the
beginning of the file.

The fseek() function clears the end-of-file flag associated
with the specified stream. Furthermore, it nullifies any prior
ungetc() on the same stream. (See ungetc().)

Related functions are ftell(), rewind(), fopen(),
fgetpos(), and fsetpos().

fsetpos

```
#include "stdio.h"
int fsetpos(FILE *stream, const fpos_t
            *position);
```

The fsetpos() function moves the file position indicator to
the point specified by the object pointed to by *position*.
This value must have been previously obtained through a
call to fgetpos(). The type fpos_t is defined in STDIO.H.
After fsetpos() is executed, the end-of-file indicator is
reset. Also, any previous call to ungetc() is nullified.

If fsetpos() fails, it returns non-zero. If it succeeds, it
returns 0.

Related functions are fgetpos(), fseek(), and ftell().

ftell

```
#include "stdio.h"
long ftell(FILE *stream);
```

The ftell() function returns the current value of the file
position indicator for the specified stream. In the case of
binary streams, the value is the number of bytes that the
indicator is away from the beginning of the file. For text
streams, the return value may not be meaningful except as
an argument to fseek() because of possible character
translations—such as carriage-return/linefeed sequences
being substituted for newline characters—that affect the
apparent size of the file.

The ftell() function returns –1L when an error occurs. If
the stream is incapable of random seeks—if it is a modem,
for instance—then the return value is undefined.

Related functions are fseek() and fgetpos().

fwrite

```
#include "stdio.h"
int fwrite(const void *buf, size_tm int
            size, size_t count, FILE *stream);
```

The fwrite() function writes *count* number of objects, each
object being *size* bytes in length, to the stream pointed to
by *stream*, from the character array pointed to by *buf*. The
file position indicator is advanced by the number of
characters written.

The fwrite() function returns the number of items actually
written, which, if the function is successful, will equal the
number requested. If fewer items are written than are
requested, then an error has occurred. For text streams,
various character translations may take place, but they will
not affect the return value.

Related functions are fread(), fscanf(), getc(), and fgetc().

getc

```
#include "stdio.h"
int getc(FILE *stream);
```

The getc() function returns the next character from the input *stream* from the current position and increments the file position indicator. The character is read as an unsigned char that is converted to an integer.

If the end of the file is reached, getc() returns EOF. However, since EOF is a valid integer value, when working with binary files, you must use feof() to check for end-of-file. If getc() encounters an error, EOF is also returned. If working with binary files, you must use ferror() to check for file errors.

The functions getc() and fgetc() are identical and, in most implementations, getc() is simply defined as the macro shown here.

```
#define getc(fp)  fgetc(fp)
```

This causes the fgetc() function to be substituted for the getc() macro.

Related functions are fputc(), fgetc(), putc(), and fopen().

getch and getche

```
#include "conio.h"
int getch(void);
int getche(void);
```

The getch() and getche() functions are not defined by the ANSI C standard. However, they are commonly included with DOS-based compilers.

The getch() function returns the next character read from the console but does not echo that character to the screen.

The **getche()** function returns the next character read from the console and echoes that character to the screen.

Both of these functions bypass C's standard I/O functions and work directly with the operating system. You can think of **getch()** and **getche()** as performing direct keyboard input.

Related functions are **getc()**, **getchar()**, and **fgetc()**.

getchar

```
#include "stdio.h"
int getchar(void);
```

The **getchar()** function returns the next character from **stdin**. The character is read as an **unsigned char** that is converted to an integer.

If the end of the file is reached, **getc()** returns **EOF**. However, since **EOF** is a valid integer value, when working with binary files, you must use **feof()** to check for end-of-file. If **getc()** encounters an error, **EOF** is also returned. If working with binary files, you must use **ferror()** to check for file errors.

The **getchar()** function is often implemented as a macro, as shown here:

```
getc(stdin)
```

Related functions are **fputc()**, **fgetc()**, **putc()**, and **fopen()**.

gets

```
#include "stdio.h"
char *gets(char *str);
```

The gets() function reads characters from stdin and places them into the character array pointed to by *str*. Characters are read until a newline character or an EOF is received. The newline character is not made part of the string; instead, it is translated into a null to terminate the string.

If successful, gets() returns *str*; a null pointer is returned upon failure. If a read error occurs, the contents of the array pointed to by *str* are indeterminate. Because a null pointer will be returned when either an error has occurred or the end of the file has been reached, you should use feof() or ferror() to determine what has actually happened.

There is no limit to the number of characters that gets() will read, and it is therefore your job to make sure that the array pointed to by *str* will not be overrun.

Related functions are fputs(), fgetc(), fgets(), and puts().

getw

```
#include "stdio.h"
int getw(FILE *stream);
```

The getw() function is not defined by the ANSI C standard, but is included with many C compilers.

The getw() function returns the next integer from *stream* and advances the file position indicator appropriately.

Because the integer read may have a value equal to EOF, you must use feof() and/or ferror() to determine when the end-of-file is reached or whether an error has occurred.

Related functions are putw() and fread().

kbhit

```
#include "conio.h"
int kbhit(void);
```

The kbhit() function is not defined by the ANSI standard. However, it is found under various names in virtually all C implementations. It returns a non-zero value if a key has been pressed at the console, and returns 0 otherwise. (Under no circumstances does it wait for a key to be pressed.) The kbhit() function does not actually read the key. You must input the key using one of C's console input functions.

Related functions are fgetc() and getc().

lseek

```
#include "io.h"
long lseek(int fd, long offset, int origin);
```

The lseek() function is part of the UNIX-like I/O system and is not defined by the ANSI C standard.

The lseek() function sets the file position indicator to the location specified by *offset* and *origin*. The *offset* is the number of bytes from *origin* to seek to. The values for *origin* must be one of these macros (defined in IO.H).

Name	Meaning
SEEK_SET	Seek from start of file
SEEK_CUR	Seek from current location
SEEK_END	Seek from end of file

The lseek() function returns *offset* on success. Upon failure, –1L is returned.

Related functions are read(), write(), open(), and close().

open

```
#include "fcntl.h"
#include "io.h"
int open(char *fname, int mode);
```

The open() function is part of the UNIX-like I/O system and is not defined by the ANSI C standard.

Unlike the ANSI I/O system, the UNIX-like system does not use file pointers of type FILE, but rather file descriptors of type int. The open() function opens a file whose name is pointed to by *fname* and sets its access mode as specified by *mode*. The values *mode* may have are shown here. (These macros are defined in FCNTL.H.)

Mode	Effect
O_RDONLY	Open for reading
O_WRONLY	Open for writing
O_RDWR	Open for reading and writing

Many compilers have additional modes such as text, binary, and the like; check your user manual.

A successful call to open() returns a positive integer that is the file descriptor associated with the file. A return value of –1 means that the file cannot be opened.

In most implementations, if the file specified in the open() statement does not appear on the disk, the operation will fail and the file will not be created. (Use the creat() function to create a new file.) However, depending upon the implementation, you may be able to use open() to create a file which is currently nonexistent. Check your user manual.

Related functions are close(), read(), write(), and creat().

perror

```
#include "stdio.h"
void perror(const char *str);
```

The perror() function maps the value of the global variable errno onto a string and writes that string to stderr. If the value of *str* is not null, then the string is written first, followed by a colon, and then the implementation-defined error message.

printf

```
#include "stdio.h"
int printf(const char *format, ...);
```

The printf() function writes to stdout the arguments that comprise the argument list as specified by the string pointed to by *format*.

The string pointed to by *format* consists of two types of items. The first type is made up of characters that will be printed on the screen. The second type contains format commands that define the way the arguments are displayed. A format command begins with a percent sign and is followed by the format code. There must be exactly the same number of arguments as there are format commands, and the format commands and the arguments are matched in order. For example, this printf() call

```
printf("Hi %c %d %s", 'c', 10, "there!");
```

displays "Hi c 10 there!".

If there are insufficient arguments with which to match the format commands, the output is undefined. If there are more arguments than format commands, then the remaining arguments are discarded. The format commands are shown here:

Code	Format
%c	Character
%d	Signed decimal integers
%i	Signed decimal integers
%e	Scientific notation (lowercase e)
%E	Scientific notation (uppercase E)
%f	Decimal floating point
%g	Uses %e or %f, whichever is shorter (if %e, uses lowercase e)
%G	Uses %E or %f, whichever is shorter (if %E, uses uppercase E)
%o	Unsigned octal
%s	String of characters
%u	Unsigned decimal integers

Code	Format
%x	Unsigned hexadecimal (lowercase letters)
%X	Unsigned hexadecimal (uppercase letters)
%p	Displays a pointer
%n	The associated argument shall be a pointer to an integer into which is placed the number of characters written so far.
%%	Prints a % sign

The `printf()` function returns the number of characters actually printed. A negative return value indicates that an error has taken place.

The format commands may have modifiers that specify the field width, the number of decimal places, and a left justification flag. An integer placed between the % sign and the format command acts as a *minimum field width specifier*. This pads the output with blanks or zeros to ensure that it is at least a certain minimum length. If the string or number is greater than that minimum, it will be printed in full even if it overruns the minimum. The default padding is done with spaces. If you wish to pad with zeros, place a 0 before the field width specifier. For example, `%05d` will pad a number of less than five digits with zeros so that its total length is five.

To specify the number of decimal places printed for a floating-point number, place a decimal point followed by the number of decimal places you wish to display after the field width specifier. For example, `%10.4f` will display a number at least ten characters wide with four decimal places. When this is applied to strings or integers, the number following the period specifies the maximum field length. For example, `%5.7s` will display a string that will be at least five characters long and will not exceed seven characters. If the string is longer than the maximum field width, the excess characters will be truncated off of the end.

By default, all output is *right-justified*: If the field width is larger than the data printed, the data will be placed on the right edge of the field. You can force the information to be left-justified by placing a minus sign directly after the %. For example, `%-10.2f` will left-justify a floating-point number with two decimal places in a ten-character field.

There are two format command modifiers that allow `printf()` to display `short` and `long` integers. These modifiers may be applied to the `d`, `i`, `o`, `u`, and `x` type specifiers. The `l` modifier tells `printf()` that a `long` data type follows. For example, `%ld` means that a `long int` is to be displayed. The `h` modifier instructs `printf()` to display a `short int`. Therefore, `%hu` indicates that the data is of type `short unsigned int`.

The `l` modifier may also prefix the floating-point commands of `e`, `f`, and `g`, indicating that a `double` follows. To output a `long double`, use the `%L` prefix.

The `%n` command causes the number of characters that have been written at the time the `%n` is encountered to be placed in an integer variable whose pointer is specified in the argument list. For example, this code fragment displays the number 14 after the line "this is a test":

```
int i;

printf("this is a test%n", &i);
printf("%d", i);
```

The `#` has a special meaning when used with some `printf()` format codes. Preceding a `g`, `f`, or `e` code with a `#` ensures that the decimal point will be present even if there are no decimal digits. If you precede the x format code with a `#`, the hexadecimal number will be printed with a

0x prefix. If you precede the o format code with a #, the octal value will be printed with a 0 prefix. The # cannot be applied to any other format specifiers.

The minimum field width and precision specifiers may be provided by arguments to printf() instead of by constants. To accomplish this, use an asterisk (*) as a placeholder. When the format string is scanned, printf() will match the *s to the arguments in the order in which they occur.

Related functions are scanf() and fprintf().

putc

```
#include "stdio.h"
int putc(int ch, FILE *stream);
```

The putc() function writes the character contained in the least significant byte of *ch* to the output stream pointed to by *stream*. Because character arguments are elevated to integer at the time of the call, you may use character variables as arguments to putc().

The putc() function returns the character written on success or EOF if an error occurs. If the output stream has been opened in binary mode, then EOF is a valid value for *ch*. This means that you must use ferror() to determine whether an error has occurred.

When implemented as a macro, the putc() function is often replaced with fputc(), because fputc() is functionally equivalent to putc().

Related functions are fgetc(), fputc(), getchar(), and putchar().

putch

```
#include "conio.h"
int putch(int ch);
```

The **putch()** function is not defined by the ANSI C standard. However, it is commonly included in the standard library of DOS-based compilers.

The **putch()** function outputs the character specified in the low-order byte of *ch* to the screen. In many implementations, its output may not be redirected. Also, in some environments, it may operate relative to a window rather than the screen.

Related functions are **putc()** and **putchar()**.

putchar

```
#include "stdio.h"
int putchar(int ch);
```

The **putchar()** function writes the character contained in the least significant byte of *ch* to **stdout**. It is functionally equivalent to **putc(ch,stdout)**. Because character arguments are elevated to integer at the time of the call, you may use character variables as arguments to **putchar()**.

The **putchar()** function returns the character written on success or **EOF** if an error occurs. If the output stream has been opened in binary mode, then **EOF** is a valid value for *ch*. This means that you must use **ferror()** to determine whether an error has occurred.

A related function is **putc()**.

puts

```
#include "stdio.h"
int puts(char *str);
```

The puts() function writes the string pointed to by *str* to the standard output device. The null terminator is translated to a newline character.

The puts() function returns a non-negative value if successful and an EOF upon failure.

Related functions are putc(), gets(), and printf().

putw

```
#include "stdio.h"
int putw(int i, FILE *stream);
```

The putw() function is not defined by the ANSI C standard, but is commonly included in the standard library.

The putw() function writes the integer *i* to *stream* at the current file position and increments the file position pointer appropriately.

The putw() function returns the value written. In text mode, a return value of EOF means that an error has occurred in the stream. Because EOF is also a valid integer value, you must use ferror() to detect an error in a binary stream.

Related functions are getw(), printf(), and fwrite().

read

```
#include "io.h"
int read(int fd, char *buf, unsigned int
         count);
```

The read() function is part of the UNIX-like I/O system and is not defined by the ANSI C standard.

The read() function reads *count* number of bytes from the file described by *fd* into the buffer pointed to by *buf*. The file position indicator is increased by the number of bytes read. If the file is opened in text mode, then character translations may take place.

The return value will be equal to the number of bytes actually read. This number may be smaller than *count* if either an end-of-file or an error is encountered. A value of –1 means an error, and 0 is returned if an attempt is made to read at end-of-file.

The read() function tends to be implementation dependent and may exhibit behavior slightly different than that described here. Check your user manual.

Related functions are open(), close(), write(), and lseek().

remove

```
#include "stdio.h"
int remove(const char *fname);
```

The remove() function erases the file specified by *fname*.

It returns 0 if the file was successfully deleted and a non-zero value if an error occurred.

A related function is rename().

rename

```
#include "stdio.h"
int rename(const char *oldfname, const *new
           fname);
```

The rename() function changes the name of the file specified by *oldfname* to *newfname*. The *newfname* must not match any existing directory entry.

The rename() function returns 0 if successful and non-zero if an error has occurred.

A related function is remove()

rewind

```
#include "stdio.h"
void rewind(FILE *stream);
```

The rewind() function moves the file position indicator to the start of the specified stream. It also clears the end-of-file and error flags associated with *stream*. It has no return value.

A related function is fseek()

scanf

```
#include "stdio.h"
int scanf(const char *format, ...);
```

The scanf() function is a general-purpose input routine that reads the stream stdin and stores the information in the variables pointed to in its argument list. It can read all of the built-in data types and automatically convert them into the proper internal format.

The control string pointed to by *format* consists of three classifications of characters:

- Format specifiers
- White-space characters
- Non-white-space characters

The input format specifiers are preceded by a % sign and tell scanf() which type of data is to be read next. The scanf() codes are matched in order, with the variables receiving the input in the argument list. For example, %s reads a string while %d reads an integer. These codes are listed in the following table.

Code	Meaning
%c	Read a single character
%d	Read a decimal integer
%i	Read a decimal integer
%e	Read a floating-point number
%f	Read a floating-point number
%g	Read a floating-point number
%o	Read an octal number

Code	Meaning
%s	Read a string
%x	Read a hexadecimal number
%p	Read a pointer
%n	Receives an integer of value equal to the number of characters read so far
%u	Read an unsigned integer
%[]	Scan for a set of characters

The format string is read left to right, and the format codes are matched, in order, with the arguments that comprise the argument list.

A white-space character in the format string causes scanf() to skip over one or more white-space characters in the input stream. A white-space character is either a space, a tab, or a newline character. In essence, one white-space character in the control string will cause scanf() to read, but not store, any number (including zero) of white-space characters up to the first non-white-space character.

A non-white-space character in the format string causes scanf() to read and discard a matching character. For example, "%d,%d" causes scanf() to first read an integer, then read and discard a comma, and finally read another integer. If the specified character is not found, scanf() will terminate.

All the variables used to receive values through scanf() must be passed by their addresses. This means that all arguments must be pointers to the variables used as arguments. This is C's way of creating a "call by reference," and it allows a function to alter the contents of an argument. For example, if you wanted to read an integer

into the variable **count**, you would use the following
scanf() call.

```
scanf("%d", &count);
```

Strings will be read into character arrays, and the array
name, without any index, is the address of the first element
of the array. So, to read a string into the character array
address, you would use

```
scanf("%s", address);
```

In this case, **address** is already a pointer and need not be
preceded by the & operator.

When reading strings, it is important to remember that
input will stop when the first white-space character is
encountered. If you want to input strings that contain
white-space characters, use a function such as **gets()**
instead.

The input data items must be separated by spaces, tabs,
or newline characters. Punctuation such as commas,
semicolons, and the like do not count as separators. This
means that

```
scanf("%d%d", &r, &c);
```

will accept an input of **10 20**, but fail with **10,20**.

When an * is placed after the % and before the format
code, it will read data of the specified type but suppress
its assignment. Thus, the following command

```
scanf("%d%*c%d", &x, &y);
```

given the input "10/20" will place the value 10 into **x**,
discard the divide sign, and give **y** the value 20.

The format commands can specify a maximum field length
modifier. This is an integer number placed between the %
and the format command code that limits the number of
characters read for any field. For example, if you wanted to
read no more than 20 characters into **address**, then you
would write

```
scanf("%20s", address);
```

If the input stream were greater than 20 characters, then a
subsequent call to input would begin where this call left
off. Input for a field may terminate before the maximum
field length is reached if a white-space character is
encountered. In this case, **scanf()** moves on to the next
field.

Although spaces, tabs, and newline characters are used as
field separators, when being read as a single character,
they are read like any other character. For example, with
an input stream of **x y**,

```
scanf("%c%c%c", &a, &b, &c);
```

will return with the character 'x' in **a**, a space in **b**, and the
character 'y' in **c**.

Be careful: Any other characters in the control string—
including spaces, tabs, and newline characters—will be
used to match and discard characters from the input
stream. Any character that matches is discarded. For
example, given the input stream "10t20",

```
scanf("%st%s", &x, &y);
```

will place 10 into **x** and 20 into **y**. The 't' is discarded
because of the 't' in the control string.

The ANSI C standard has added a new feature to **scanf()**
that was not part of the original UNIX version, called a

scanset. A scanset defines a set of characters that may be read by scanf() and assigned to the corresponding character array. You define a scanset by putting a string of the characters you want to scan for inside square brackets. The beginning square bracket must be prefixed by a percent sign. For example, this scanset:

```
% [ABC]
```

tells scanf() to read only the characters A, B, and C.

When a scanset is used, scanf() continues to read characters and put them into the corresponding character array until a character that is not in the scanset is encountered. The corresponding variable must be a pointer to a character array. Upon return from scanf(), the array will contain a null-terminated string comprised of the characters read.

You can specify an inverted set if the first character in the set is a caret (^). When the ^ is present, it instructs scanf() to accept any character that *is not* defined by the scanset.

You can specify a range with a hyphen. For example, the following command tells scanf() to accept the characters A through Z.

```
% [A-Z]
```

One important point to remember is that the scanset is case-sensitive. Therefore, if you want to scan for both upper- and lowercase letters, they must be specified individually.

The scanf() function returns a number equal to the number of fields that were successfully assigned values. This number will not include fields that were read but not assigned because the * modifier was used to suppress the assignment. EOF is returned if an error occurs before the first field is assigned.

Related functions are printf() and fscanf().

setbuf

```
#include "stdio.h"
void setbuf(FILE *stream, char *buf);
```

The setbuf() function is used to either specify the buffer the specified stream will use, or, if called with *buf* set to null, to turn off buffering. If a programmer-defined buffer is to be specified, then it must be BUFSIZ characters long. BUFSIZ is defined in STDIO.H.

The setbuf() function does not return a value.

Related functions are fopen(), fclose(), and setvbuf().

setvbuf

```
#include "stdio.h"
int setvbuf(FILE *stream, char *buf, int
            mode, size_t size);
```

The setvbuf() function allows the programmer to specify the buffer, its size, and its mode for the specified stream. The character array pointed to by *buf* is used as *stream*'s buffer for I/O operations. The size of the buffer is set by *size*, and *mode* determines how buffering will be handled. If *buf* is null, setvbuf() will allocate its own buffer.

The legal values of *mode* are _IOFBF, _IONBF, and _IOLBF. These are defined in STDIO.H. When *mode* is set to _IOFBF, full buffering will take place. If *mode* is _IOLBF, then the stream will be line-buffered, which means that the buffer will be flushed each time a newline character is written for output streams. For input streams, an input request reads all characters up to a newline character. In either case, the buffer is also flushed when full. If *mode* is _IONBF, then no buffering takes place.

The value of *size* must be greater than zero.

The setvbuf() function returns 0 on success, non-zero on failure.

A related function is setbuf().

sprintf

```
#include "stdio.h"
int sprintf(char *buf, const char *format,
            ...);
```

The sprintf() function is identical to printf() except that the output is put into the array pointed to by *buf* instead of being written to the console. See the printf() section for details.

The return value is equal to the number of characters actually placed into the array.

Related functions are printf() and fsprintf().

sscanf

```
#include "stdio.h"
int sscanf(const char *buf, const char
          *format, ...);
```

The sscanf() function is identical to scanf() except that data is read from the array pointed to by *buf* rather than stdin. See scanf() for details.

The return value is equal to the number of variables that were actually assigned values. This number does not include fields that were skipped through the use of the * format command modifier. A value of 0 means that no fields were assigned, and EOF indicates that an error occurred prior to the first assignment.

Related functions are scanf() and fscanf().

tell

```
#include "io.h"
long tell(int fd);
```

The tell() function is part of the UNIX-like I/O system and is not defined by the ANSI C standard.

The tell() function returns the current value of the file position indicator associated with the file descriptor *fd*. This value will be the number of bytes the position indicator is from the start of the file. A return value of –1L indicates an error.

Related functions are ftell(), lseek(), open(), close(), read(), and write().

tmpfile

```
#include "stdio.h"
FILE *tmpfile(void);
```

The tmpfile() function opens a temporary file for update and returns a pointer to the stream. The function automatically uses a unique filename to avoid conflicts with existing files.

The tmpfile() function returns a null pointer on failure; otherwise, it returns a pointer to the stream.

The temporary file created by tmpfile() is automatically removed when the file is closed or when the program terminates.

A related function is tmpnam().

tmpnam

```
#include "stdio.h"
char *tmpnam(char *name);
```

The tmpnam() function generates a unique filename and stores it in the array pointed to by *name*. The main purpose of tmpnam() is to generate a temporary filename that is different from any other file in the current disk directory.

The function may be called up to TMP_MAX times. TMP_MAX is defined in STDIO.H. The ANSI C standard states that it will be at least 25. Each time tmpnam() is called, it will generate a new temporary filename.

A pointer to *string* is returned on success; otherwise, a null pointer is returned.

A related function is tmpfile().

ungetc

```
#include "stdio.h"
int ungetc(int ch, FILE *stream);
```

The ungetc() function returns the character specified by the low-order byte of *ch* to the input stream *stream*. This character will then be returned by the next read operation on *stream*. A call to fflush() or fseek() undoes an ungetc() operation and discards the character.

A one-character push-back is guaranteed; some implementations will accept more.

You may not unget an EOF.

A call to ungetc() clears the end-of-file flag associated with the specified stream. The value of the file position indicator for a text stream is undefined until all pushed-back characters are read, in which case it will be the same as it was prior to the first ungetc() call. For binary streams, each ungetc() call decrements the file position indicator.

The return value is equal to *ch* on success and EOF on failure.

A related function is getc().

unlink

```
#include "io.h"
int unlink(const char *fname);
```

The unlink() function is part of the UNIX-like I/O system and is not defined by the ANSI standard.

The unlink() function removes the specified file from the directory. It returns 0 on success and –1 on failure.

Related functions are open() and close().

vprintf, vfprintf, and vsprintf

```
#include "stdarg.h"
#include "stdio.h"
int vprintf(char *format, va_list arg_ptr);
int vfprintf(FILE *stream, const char
            *format, va_list arg_ptr);
int vsprintf(char *buf, char *format,
            va_list arg_ptr);
```

The functions vprintf(), vfprintf(), and vsprintf() are functionally equivalent to printf(), fprintf(), and sprintf(), respectively, except that the argument list has been replaced by a pointer to a list of arguments. This pointer must be of type va_list and is defined in STDARG.H.

Related functions are va_list(), va_start(), and va_end().

write

```
#include "io.h"
int write(int fd, char *buf, unsigned count);
```

The write() function is part of the UNIX-like I/O system and is not defined by the ANSI standard.

The write() function writes *count* number of bytes to the file described by *fd* from the buffer pointed to by *buf*. The file position indicator is increased by the number of bytes written. If the file is opened in text mode, character translations may take place.

The return value will be equal to the number of bytes actually written. This number may be smaller than *count* if an error is encountered. A value of −1 means an error has occurred.

The write() function tends to be implementation dependent and may exhibit behavior slightly different than that described here. Check your user manual.

Related functions are read(), close(), write(), and lseek().

String and Character Functions

The C standard library has a rich and varied set of string- and character-handling functions. In C, a string is a null-terminated array of characters. In a standard implementation, the string functions require the header file STRING.H to provide their prototypes. The character functions use CTYPE.H as their header file. It is possible that these files will have different names if the compiler does not follow the ANSI C standard or the old UNIX standard.

Because C has no bounds-checking on array operations, it is the programmer's responsibility to prevent an array overflow. As the ANSI C standard puts it, if an array has overflowed, "the behavior is undefined," which is a nice way of saying that your program is about to crash!

In C, a *printable character* is one that can be displayed on a terminal. These are usually the characters between a space (0x20) and a tilde (0xfE). *Control characters* have values between 0 and 0x1F as well as DEL (0x7F).

For historical reasons, the arguments to the character functions have integer values. However, only the low-order byte is used; the character function automatically converts the argument to unsigned char. Nevertheless, you are free to call these functions with character arguments, because characters are automatically elevated to integers at the time of the call.

The header file STRING.H defines the size_t type, which is essentially the same   unsigned.

isalnum

```
#include "ctype.h"
int isalnum(int ch);
```

The isalnum() function returns non-zero if its argument is either a letter of the alphabet or a digit. If the character is not alphanumeric, then 0 is returned.

Related functions are isalpha(), iscntrl(), isdigit(), isgraph(), isprint(), ispunct(), and isspace().

isalpha

```
#include "ctype.h"
int isalpha(int ch);
```

The isalpha() function returns non-zero if *ch* is a letter of the alphabet; otherwise, 0 is returned. What symbols constitute letters of the alphabet may vary from language to language. For English, these are the upper- and lowercase letters *A* through *Z*.

Related functions are isalnum(), iscntrl(), isdigit(), isgraph(), isprint(), ispunct(), and isspace().

iscntrl

```
#include "ctype.h"
int iscntrl(int ch);
```

The iscntrl() function returns non-zero if *ch* is between 0 and 0x1F or if *ch* is equal to 0x7F (DEL); otherwise, 0 is returned.

Related functions are isalnum(), isalpha(), isdigit(), isgraph(), isprint(), ispunct(), and isspace().

isdigit

```
#include "ctype.h"
int isdigit(int ch);
```

The isdigit() function returns non-zero if *ch* is a digit, that is, '0' through '9'. Otherwise, 0 is returned.

Related functions are isalnum(), isalpha(), iscntrl(), isgraph(), isprint(), ispunct(), and isspace().

isgraph

```
#include "ctype.h"
int isgraph(int ch);
```

The isgraph() function returns non-zero if *ch* is any printable character other than a space; otherwise, 0 is returned. Although implementation dependent, printable characters are generally in the range 0x21 through 0x7E.

Related functions are isalnum(), isalpha(), iscntrl(), isdigit(), isprint(), ispunct(), and isspace().

islower

```
#include "ctype.h"
int islower(int ch);
```

The islower() function returns non-zero if *ch* is a lowercase letter; otherwise, 0 is returned.

A related function is isupper().

isprint

```
#include "ctype.h"
int isprint(int ch);
```

The isprint() function returns non-zero if *ch* is a printable character, including a space; otherwise, 0 is returned. Although implementation dependent, printable characters are often in the range 0x20 through 0x7E.

Related functions are isalnum(), isalpha(), iscntrl(), isdigit(), isgraph(), ispunct(), and isspace().

ispunct

```
#include "ctype.h"
int ispunct(int ch);
```

The ispunct() function returns non-zero if *ch* is a punctuation character; otherwise, 0 is returned. The term *punctuation*, as defined by this function, includes all printing characters that are neither alphanumeric nor a space.

Related functions are isalnum(), isalpha(), iscntrl(), isdigit(), isgraph(), and isspace().

isspace

```
#include "ctype.h"
int isspace(int ch);
```

The isspace() function returns non-zero if *ch* is a space, horizontal tab, vertical tab, form feed, carriage return or newline character; otherwise, 0 is returned.

Related functions are isalnum(), isalpha(), iscntrl(), isdigit(), isgraph(), and ispunct().

isupper

```
#include "ctype.h"
int isupper(int ch);
```

The isupper() function returns non-zero if *ch* is an uppercase letter; otherwise, 0 is returned.

A related function is islower().

isxdigit

```
#include "ctype.h"
int isxdigit(int ch);
```

The isxdigit() function returns non-zero if *ch* is a hexadecimal digit; otherwise, 0 is returned. A hexadecimal digit will be in one of these ranges: A-F, a-f, or 0-9.

Related functions are isalnum(), isalpha(), iscntrl(), isdigit(), isgraph(), ispunct(), and isspace()

memchr

```
#include "string.h"
void *memchr(const void *buffer, int ch,
              size_t count);
```

The memchr() function searches the array pointed to by *buffer* for the first occurrence of *ch* in the first *count* characters.

The memchr() function returns a pointer to the first occurrence of *ch* in *buffer*, or a null pointer if *ch* is not found.

Related functions are memcpy() and isspace().

memcmp

```
#include "string.h"
int memcmp(const void *buf1, const void
            *buf2, size_t count);
```

The memcmp() function compares the first *count* characters of the arrays pointed to by *buf1* and *buf2*. The comparison is done lexicographically.

The memcmp() function returns an integer that is interpreted as indicated here.

Value	Meaning
Less than 0	*buf1* is less than *buf2*
0	*buf1* is equal to *buf2*
Greater than 0	*buf1* is greater than *buf2*

Related functions are memchr(), memcpy(), and strcmp().

memcpy

```
#include "string.h"
void *memcpy(void *to, const void *from,
             size_t count);
```

The memcpy() function copies *count* characters from the array pointed to by *from* into the array pointed to by *to*. If the arrays overlap, the behavior of memcopy() is undefined.

The memcpy() function returns a pointer to *to*.

A related function is memmove().

memmove

```
#include "string.h"
void *memmove(void *to, const void *from,
              size_t count);
```

The memmove() function copies *count* characters from the array pointed to by *from* into the array pointed to by *to*. If the arrays overlap, the copy will take place correctly, placing the correct contents into *to* but leaving *from* modified.

The memmove() function returns a pointer to *to*.

A related function is memcpy().

memset

```
#include "string.h"
void *memset(void *buf, int ch, size_t
             count);
```

The memset() function copies the low-order byte of *ch* into the first *count* characters of the array pointed to by *buf*. It returns *buf*.

The most common use of memset() is to initialize a region of memory to some known value.

Related functions are memcmp(), memcpy(), and memmove().

strcat

```
#include "string.h"
char *strcat(char *str1, const char *str2);
```

The strcat() function concatenates a copy of *str2* to *str1* and terminates *str1* with a null. The null terminator originally ending *str1* is overwritten by the first character of *str2*. The string *str2* is untouched by the operation. If the arrays overlap, the behavior of strcat() is undefined.

The strcat() function returns *str1*.

Remember, no bounds-checking takes place, so it is the programmer's responsibility to ensure that *str1* is large enough to hold both its original contents and those of *str2*.

Related functions are strchr(), strcmp(), and strcpy().

strchr

```
#include "string.h"
char *strchr(const char *str, int ch);
```

The strchr() function returns a pointer to the first occurrence of the low-order byte of *ch* in the string pointed to by *str*. If no match is found, a null pointer is returned.

Related functions are strpbrk(), strspn (), strstr(), and strtok().

strcoll

```
#include "string.h"
int strcoll(const char *str1, const char
            *str2);
```

The strcoll() function compares the string pointed to by *str1* with the one pointed to by *str2*. The comparison is performed in accordance with the locale specified using the setlocale() function. (See setlocale() for details.)

The strcoll() function returns an integer that is interpreted as indicated here.

Value	Meaning
Less than 0	*str1* is less than *str2*
0	*str1* is equal to *str2*
Greater than 0	*str1* is greater than *str2*

Related functions are memcmp() and strcmp().

strcmp

```
#include "string.h"
int strcmp(const char *str1, const char
          *str2);
```

The strcmp() function lexicographically compares two strings and returns an integer based on the outcome, as shown here.

Value	Meaning
Less than 0	*str1* is less than *str2*
0	*str1* is equal to *str2*
Greater than 0	*str1* is greater than *str2*

Related functions are strchr(), strcpy(), and strncmp().

strcpy

```
#include "string.h"
char *strcpy(char *str1, const char *str2);
```

The strcpy() function is used to copy the contents of *str2* into *str1*. *str2* must be a pointer to a null-terminated string. The strcpy() function returns a pointer to *str1*.

If *str1* and *str2* overlap, the behavior of strcpy() is undefined.

Related functions are memcpy(), strchr(), strcmp(), and strncmp().

strcspn

```
#include "string.h"
int strcspn(const char *str1, const *str2);
```

The strcspn() function returns the length of the initial substring of the string pointed to by *str1* that is made up of only those characters not contained in the string pointed to by *str2*. Stated differently, strcspn() returns the index of the first character in the string pointed to by *str1* that matches any of the characters in the string pointed to by *str2*.

Related functions are strpbrk(), strrchr(), strstr(), and strtok().

strerror

```
#include "string.h"
char *strerror(int errnum);
```

The strerror() function returns a pointer to an implementation-defined string which is associated with the value of *errnum*. Under no circumstances should you modify the string.

strlen

```
#include "string.h"
size_t strlen(char *str);
```

The strlen() function returns the length of the null-terminated string pointed to by *str*. The null is not counted.

Related functions are memcpy(), strchr(), strcmp(), and strncmp().

strncat

```
#include "string.h"
char *strncat(char *str1, const *str2,
              size_t count);
```

The strncat() function concatenates not more than *count* characters of the string pointed to by *str2* to the string pointed to by *str1*, and it terminates *str1* with a null. The null terminator originally ending *str1* is overwritten by the first character of *str2*. The string *str2* is untouched by the operation. If the strings overlap, the behavior is undefined.

The strncat() function returns *str1*.

Remember, no bounds-checking takes place, so it is the programmer's responsibility to ensure that *str1* is large enough to hold both its original contents and those of *str2*.

Related functions are strcat(), strnchr(), strncmp(), and strncpy().

strncmp

```
#include "string.h"
int strncmp(const char *str1, const char
          *str2, size_t count);
```

The strncmp() function lexicographically compares not more than *count* characters from the two null-terminated strings and returns an integer based on the outcome, as shown here.

Value	Meaning
Less than 0	*str1* is less than *str2*
0	*str1* is equal to *str2*
Greater than 0	*str1* is greater than *str2*

If there are less than *count* characters in either string then the comparison ends when the first null is encountered.

Related functions are strcmp(), strnchr(), and strncpy().

strncpy

```
#include "string.h"
char *strncpy(char *str1, const char *str2,
             size_t count);
```

The strncpy() function is used to copy up to *count* characters from the string pointed to by *str2* into the string pointed to by *str1*. *str2* must be a pointer to a null-terminated string. The strncpy() function returns a pointer to *str1*.

If *str1* and *str2* overlap, the behavior of **strncpy()** is undefined.

If the string pointed to by *str2* has less than *count* characters, then nulls will be appended to the end of *str1* until *count* characters have been copied.

Alternately, if the string pointed to by *str2* is longer than *count* characters, then the resultant string pointed to by *str1* will not be null-terminated.

The **strncpy()** function returns a pointer to *str1*.

Related functions are **memcpy()**, **strchr()**, **strncat()**, and **strncmp()**.

strpbrk

```
#include "string.h"
char *strpbrk(const char *str1, const char
              *str2);
```

The **strpbrk()** function returns a pointer to the first character in the string pointed to by *str1* that matches any character in the string pointed to by *str2*. The null terminators are not included. If there are no matches, a null pointer is returned.

Related functions are **strrchr()**, **strspn()**, **strstr()**, and **strtok()**.

strrchr

```
#include "string.h"
char *strrchr(const char *str, int ch);
```

The strrchr() function returns a pointer to the last occurrence of the low-order byte of *ch* in the string pointed to by *str*. If no match is found, a null pointer is returned.

Related functions are strpbrk(), strspn(), strstr(), and strtok().

strspn

```
#include "string.h"
size_t strspn(const char *str1, const char
              *str2);
```

The strspn() function returns the length of the initial substring of the string pointed to by *str1* that is made up of only those characters contained in the string pointed to by *str2*. Stated differently, strspn() returns the index of the first character in the string pointed to by *str1* that does not match any of the characters in the string pointed to by *str2*.

Related functions are strpbrk(), strrchr(), strstr(), and strtok().

strstr

```
#include "string.h"
char *strstr(const char *str1, const char
             *str2);
```

The strstr() function returns a pointer to the first occurrence in the string pointed to by *str1* of the string pointed to by *str2*. It returns a null pointer if no match is found.

Related functions are **strchr()**, **strcspn()**, **strpbrk()**, **strrchr()**, **strspn()**, and **strtok()**.

strtok

```
#include "string.h"
char *strtok(char *str1, const char *str2);
```

The **strtok()** function returns a pointer to the next token in the string pointed to by *str1*. The characters making up the string pointed to by *str2* are the delimiters which may terminate the token. A null pointer is returned when there is no token to return.

The first time **strtok()** is called, *str1* is actually used in the call. Subsequent calls must use a null pointer for the first argument.

It is important to understand that the **strtok()** function modifies the string pointed to by *str1*. Each time a token is found, a null is placed where the delimiter was found. In this way, **strtok()** can continue to advance through the string.

It is possible to use a different set of delimiters for each call to **strtok()**.

Related functions are **strchr()**, **strcspn()**, **strpbrk()**, **strrchr()**, and **strspn()**.

strxfrm

```
#include "string.h"
size_t strxfrm(char *str1, const char *str2,
                size_t count);
```

The strxfrm() function transforms the first *count* characters of the string pointed to by *str2* so that they can be used by the strcmp() function and puts the result into the string pointed to by *str1*. After the transformation, the outcome of a strcmp() using *str1* and a strcoll() using the original string pointed to by *str2* will be the same. This function is mainly used in foreign language environments that do not use the ASCII collating sequence.

The strxfrm() function returns the length of the transformed string.

A related function is strcoll().

tolower

```
#include "ctype.h"
int tolower(int ch);
```

The tolower() function returns the lowercase equivalent of *ch* if *ch* is a letter; otherwise, *ch* is returned unchanged.

A related function is toupper().

toupper

```
#include "ctype.h"
int toupper(int ch);
```

The toupper() function returns the uppercase equivalent of *ch* if *ch* is a letter; otherwise, *ch* is returned unchanged.

A related function is tolower().

Mathematical Functions

The ANSI C standard defines 22 mathematical functions, which fall into the following categories:

- Trigonometric functions

- Hyperbolic functions

- Exponential and logarithmic functions

- Miscellaneous

Even if your compiler is not completely standard, the math functions described here will most likely be applicable.

All of the math functions require the header MATH.H to be included in any program using them. In addition to declaring the math functions, this header defines three macros called EDOM, ERANGE, and HUGE_VAL. If an argument to a math function is not in the domain for which it is defined, then an implementation-defined value is returned, and the built-in global integer variable errno is set equal to EDOM. If a routine produces a result that is too large to be represented by a double, an overflow occurs. This causes the routine to return HUGE_VAL and set errno to ERANGE, indicating a range error. If an underflow happens, the routine returns 0 and sets errno to ERANGE. If your compiler does not agree with the ANSI standard, the exact operation of the routines in error situations may be different.

acos

```
#include "math.h"
double acos(double arg);
```

The **acos()** function returns the arc cosine of *arg*. The argument to **acos()** must be in the range –1 to 1; otherwise, a domain error will occur.

Related functions are **asin()**, **atan()**, **atan2()**, **sin()**, **cos()**, **tan()**, **sinh()**, **cosh()**, and **tanh()**.

asin

```
#include "math.h"
double asin(double arg);
```

The **asin()** function returns the arc sine of *arg*. The argument to **asin()** must be in the range –1 to 1; otherwise, a domain error will occur.

Related functions are **acos()**, **atan()**, **atan2()**, **sin()**, **cos()**, **tan()**, **sinh()**, **cosh()**, and **tanh()**.

atan

```
#include "math.h"
double atan(double arg);
```

The **atan()** function returns the arc tangent of *arg*.

Related functions are **asin()**, **acos()**, **atan2()**, **tan()**, **cos()**, **sin()**, **sinh()**, **cosh()**, and **tanh()**.

atan2

```
#include "math.h"
double atan2(double y, double x);
```

The atan2() function returns the arc tangent of *y/x*. It uses the signs of its arguments to compute the quadrant of the return value.

Related functions are asin(), acos(), atan(), tan(), cos(), sin(), sinh(), cosh(), and tanh().

ceil

```
#include "math.h"
double ceil(double num);
```

The ceil() function returns the smallest integer (represented as a double) not less than *num*. For example, given 1.02, ceil() would return 2.0. Given –1.02, ceil() would return –1.

Related functions are floor() and fmod().

cos

```
#include "math.h"
double cos(double arg);
```

The cos() function returns the cosine of *arg*. The value of *arg* must be given in radians.

Related functions are asin(), acos(), atan2(), atan(), tan(), sin(), sinh(), cosh(), and tanh().

cosh

```
#include "math.h"
double cosh(double arg);
```

The cosh() function returns the hyperbolic cosine of *arg*. The value of *arg* must be given in radians.

Related functions are asin(), acos(), atan2(), atan(), tan(), sin(), cos(), and tanh().

exp

```
#include "math.h"
double exp(double arg);
```

The exp() function returns the natural logarithm e raised to the *arg* power.

A related function is log().

fabs

```
#include "math.h"
double fabs(double num);
```

The fabs() function returns the absolute value of *num*.

A related function is abs().

floor

```
#include "math.h"
double floor(double num);
```

The floor() function returns the largest integer (represented as a double) not greater than *num*. For example, given 1.02, floor() would return 1.0. Given –1.02, floor() would return –2.0.

Related functions are **fceil()** and **fmod()**.

fmod

```
#include "math.h"
double fmod(double x, double y);
```

The fmod() function returns the remainder of *x/y*.

Related functions are ceil(), floor(), and fabs().

frexp

```
#include "math.h"
double frexp(double num, int *exp);
```

The frexp() function decomposes the number *num* into a mantissa in the range 0.5 to less than 1, and an integer exponent such that *num = mantissa * 2^{exp}*. The mantissa is returned by the function, and the exponent is stored at the variable pointed to by *exp*.

A related function is ldexp().

ldexp

```
#include "math.h"
double ldexp(double num, int exp);
```

The **ldexp()** function returns the value of *num* * 2^{exp}. If overflow occurs, **HUGE_VAL** is returned.

Related functions are **frexp()** and **modf()**.

log

```
#include "math.h"
double log(double num);
```

The **log()** function returns the natural logarithm for *num*. A domain error occurs if *num* is negative, and a range error occurs if the argument is 0.

A related function is **log10()**.

log10

```
#include "math.h"
double log10(double num);
```

The **log10()** function returns the base 10 logarithm for *num*. A domain error occurs if *num* is negative, and a range error occurs if the argument is 0.

A related function is **log()**.

modf

```
#include "math.h"
double modf(double num, int *i);
```

The **modf()** function decomposes *num* into its integer and fractional parts. It returns the fractional portion and places the integer part in the variable pointed to by *i*.

Related functions are **frexp()** and **ldexp()**.

pow

```
#include "math.h"
double pow(double base, double exp);
```

The **pow()** function returns *base* raised to the *exp* power ($base^{exp}$). A domain error occurs if *base* is 0 and *exp* is less than or equal to 0. An error will also happen if *base* is negative and *exp* is not an integer. An overflow produces a range error.

Related functions are **exp()**, **log()**, and **sqrt()**.

sin

```
#include "math.h"
double sin(double arg);
```

The **sin()** function returns the sine of *arg*. The value of *arg* must be given in radians.

Related functions are asin(), acos(), atan2(), atan(), tan(), cos(), sinh(), cosh(), and tanh().

sinh

```
#include "math.h"
double sinh(double arg);
```

The sinh() function returns the hyperbolic sine of *arg*. The value of *arg* must be given in radians.

Related functions are asin(), acos(), atan2(), atan(), tan(), cos(), tanh(), cosh(), and sin().

sqrt

```
#include "math.h"
double sqrt(double num);
```

The sqrt() function returns the square root of *num*. If it is called with a negative argument, a domain error will occur.

Related functions are exp(), log(), and pow().

tan

```
#include "math.h"
double tan(double arg);
```

The tan() function returns the tangent of *arg*. The value of *arg* must be given in radians.

Related functions are acos(), asin(), atan(), atan2(), cos(), sin(), sinh(), cosh(), and tanh().

tanh

```
#include "math.h"
double tanh(double arg);
```

The tanh() function returns the hyperbolic tangent of *arg*. The value of *arg* must be given in radians.

Related functions are acos(), asin(), atan(), atan2(), cos(), sin(), cosh(), sinh(), and tan().

Time, Date, and Other System-Related Functions

This section covers those functions that in one way or another are more sensitive to the operating system than are others. These include the time and date functions and those functions that relate to the geographical location in which the computer is used.

The ANSI C standard defines several functions that deal with the system date and time as well as elapsed time. These functions require the header TIME.H. This header defines three types: clock_t, time_t, and tm. The types clock_t and time_t are capable of representing the system time and date as a long integer. The ANSI C standard refers to this as *calendar time*. The structure type tm holds the date and time broken down into their elements. The tm structure is defined as shown here.

```
struct tm {
   int tm_sec;   /* seconds, 0-59 */
   int tm_min;   /* minutes, 0-59 */
   int tm_hour;  /* hours, 0-23 */
   int tm_mday;  /* day of the month, 1-31 */
   int tm_mon;   /* months since Jan, 0-11 */
   int tm_year;  /* years from 1900 */
   int tm_wday;  /* days since Sunday, 0-6 */
   int tm_yday;  /* days since Jan 1, 0-365 */
   int tm_isdst  /* Daylight Savings Time
                    indicator */
}
```

The value of tm_isdst will be positive if daylight savings time is in effect, 0 if it is not in effect, and negative if there is no information available. The ANSI C standard refers to this form of the time and date as *broken-down time*.

In addition, TIME.H defines the macro **CLK_TCK** which is the number of system clock ticks per second.

The geographical location functions require the header LOCALE.H.

Most C compilers will also supply operating system and computer-specific functions; check your compiler's user manual for these types of functions.

asctime

```
#include "time.h"
char *asctime(struct tm *ptr);
```

The **asctime()** function returns a pointer to a string. The string converts the information stored in the structure pointed to by *ptr* into the following form:

day month date hours:minutes:seconds year\n\0

For example:

Wed Jun 19 12:05:34 1999

The structure pointer passed to **asctime()** is generally obtained from either **localtime()** or **gmtime()**.

The buffer used by **asctime()** to hold the formatted output string is a statically allocated character array and is overwritten each time the function is called. If you wish to save the contents of the string, you must copy it elsewhere.

Related functions are **localtime()**, **gmtime()**, **time()**, and **ctime()**.

clock

```
#include "time.h"
clock_t clock(void);
```

The **clock()** function returns a value that represents the amount of time that the calling program has been running. To transform this value into seconds, divide it by **CLK_TCK** A value of –1 is returned if the time is not available.

Related functions are **time()**, **asctime()**, and **ctime()**.

ctime

```
#include "time.h"
char *ctime(const time_t *time);
```

The **ctime()** function returns a pointer to a string of the form:

day month year hours:minutes:seconds year\n\0

given a pointer to the calendar time. The calendar time is generally obtained through a call to **time()**.

The buffer used by **ctime()** to hold the formatted output string is a statically allocated character array and is overwritten each time the function is called. If you wish to save the contents of the string, you must copy it elsewhere.

Related functions are **localtime()**, **gmtime()**, **time()**, and **asctime()**.

difftime

```
#include "time.h"
double difftime(time_t time2, time_t time1);
```

The **difftime()** function returns the difference, in seconds, between *time1* and *time2*. That is, it returns *time2 – time1*.

Related functions are localtime(), gmtime(), time(), and asctime().

gmtime

```
#include "time.h"
struct tm *gmtime(time_t *time);
```

The **gmtime()** function returns a pointer to the broken-down form of *time* in the form of a **tm** structure. The time is represented in Greenwich mean time. The *time* value is generally obtained through a call to time().

The structure used by **gmtime()** to hold the broken-down time is statically allocated and is overwritten each time the function is called. If you wish to save the contents of the structure, you must copy it elsewhere.

Related functions are localtime(), time(), and asctime().

localeconv

```
#include "locale.h"
struct lconv *localeconv(void);
```

The localeconv() function returns a pointer to a structure
of type lconv that contains various country-specific
environmental information relating to the way numbers are
formatted. The lconv structure is organized as shown here.

```
struct lconv {
  char *decimal_point; /* decimal point char-
                          acter for non-mone-
                          tary values */
  char *thousands_sep; /* thousands separator
                          for non-monetary
                          values */
  char *grouping; /* specifies grouping for
                     non-monetary values */
  char int_curr_symbol; /* international cur-
                           rency symbol */
  char *currency_symbol; /* local currency
                            symbol */
  char *mon_decimal_point; /* decimal point
                              character for
                              monetary
                              values */
  char *mon_thousands_sep; /* thousands sep-
                              arator for
                              monetary
                              values */
  char *mon_grouping; /* specifies grouping
                         for monetary
                         values */
  char *positive_sign; /* positive value in-
                          dicator for mone-
                          tary values */
  char *negative_sign; /* negative value in-
                          dicator for mone-
                          tary values */
  char int_frac_digits; /* number of digits
                           displayed to the
                           right of the deci-
                           mal point for mon-
                           etary values
                           displayed using
```

```
                               international
                               format */
      char frac_digits; /* number of digits dis-
                           played to the right
                           of the decimal point
                           for monetary values
                           displayed using local
                           format */
      char p_cs_precedes; /* 1 if currency sym-
                             bol precedes posi-
                             tive value, 0 if
                             currency symbol
                             follows value *.
      char p_sep_by_space; /* 1 if currency sym-
                              bol is separated
                              from value by a
                              space, 0 otherwise
                              */
      char n_cs_precedes; /* 1 if currency sym-
                             bol precedes a nega-
                             tive value, 0 if
                             currency symbol fol-
                             lows value */
      char n_sep_by_space; /* 1 if currency sym-
                              bol is separated
                              from a negative
                              value by a space,
                              0 if currency sym-
                              bol follows value
                              */
      char p_sign_posn; /* indicates position of
                           positive value symbol
                           */
      char n_sign_posn; /* indicates position of
                           negative value symbol
                           */
}
```

The `localeconv()` function returns a pointer to the `conv`
structure. You must not alter the contents of this structure.

Refer to your compiler manual for implementation-specific information relating to this function.

A related function is setlocale().

localtime

```
#include "time.h"
struct tm *localtime(const time_t *time);
```

The localtime() function returns a pointer to the broken-down form of *time* in the form of a tm structure. The time is represented in local time. The *time* value is generally obtained through a call to time().

The structure used by localtime() to hold the broken-down time is statically allocated and is overwritten each time the function is called. If you wish to save the contents of the structure, you must copy it elsewhere.

Related functions are gmtime(), time(), and asctime().

mktime

```
#include "time.h"
time_t mktime(struct tm *time);
```

The mktime() function returns the calendar time equivalent of the broken-down time found in the structure pointed to by *time*. This function is primarily used to initialize the system time. The elements tm_wday and tm_yday are set by the function, so they need not be defined at the time of the call.

If mktime() cannot represent the information as a valid calendar time, –1 is returned.

Related functions are time(), gmtime(), asctime(), and ctime().

setlocale

```
#include "locale.h"
char *setlocale(int type, const char
                *locale);
```

The setlocale() function allows certain parameters that reflect the geopolitical location of a program's execution to be queried or set. In Europe, for example, monetary values have a comma where a decimal point would be used in the United States.

If *locale* is null, then setlocale() returns a pointer to the current localization string. Otherwise, setlocale() attempts to use the specified localization string to set the locale parameters as specified by *type*.

At the time of the call, *type* must be one of the following macros:

LC_ALL
LC_COLLATE
LC_CTYPE
LC_MONETARY
LC_NUMERIC
LC_TIME

LC_ALL refers to all localization categories.
LC_COLLATE affects the operation of the strcoll() function. LC_CTYPE alters the way the character functions work. LC_MONETARY determines the

monetary format. LC_NUMERIC changes the
decimal-point character for formatted input/output
functions. Finally, LC_TIME determines the behavior of
the strftime() function.

The ANSI C standard defines two possible strings for
locale. The first is "C", which specifies a minimal
environment for C compilation. The second is " ", the
null string, which specifies the implementation-defined
default environment. All other values for *locale* are
implementation-defined and will affect portability.

The setlocale() function returns a pointer to a string
associated with the *type* parameter.

Related functions are localeconv(), time(), strcoll(), and
strftime()

strftime

```
#include "time.h"
size_t strftime(char *str, size_t maxsize,
                char const *fmt,
                const struct tm *time);
```

The strftime() function places time, date, and other
information into the string pointed to by *str* according to
the format commands found in the string pointed to by *fmt*,
using the broken-down time *time*. A maximum of *maxsize*
characters will be placed into *str*.

The strftime() function works a little like sprintf() in that
it recognizes a set of format commands that begin with the
percent sign (%) and it places its formatted output into a
string. The format commands are used to specify the exact
way that various time and date information is represented
in *str*. Any other characters found in the format string are

placed into *str* unchanged. The time and date displayed are in local time. The format commands are shown in the following table. Notice that many of the commands are case-sensitive.

Command	Replaced by
%a	Abbreviated weekday name
%A	Full weekday name
%b	Abbreviated month name
%B	Full month name
%c	Standard date and time string
%d	Day-of-month as a decimal (1-31)
%H	Hour (0-23)
%I	Hour (1-12)
%j	Day-of-year as a decimal (1-366)
%m	Month as decimal (1-12)
%M	Minute as decimal (0-59)
%p	Locale's equivalent of AM or PM
%S	Second as decimal (0-59)
%U	Week-of-year, Sunday being first day (0-52)
%w	Weekday as a decimal (0-6, Sunday being 0)
%W	Week-of-year, Monday being first day (0-52)
%x	Standard date string
%X	Standard time string
%y	Year in decimal without century (00-99)
%Y	Year including century as decimal
%Z	Time zone name
%%	The percent sign

The strftime() function returns the number of characters placed in the string pointed to by *str*, or 0 if an error occurs.

Related functions are time(), localtime(), and gmtime().

time

```
#include "time.h"
time_t time(time_t *time);
```

The **time()** function returns the current calendar time of the system. If the system has no time, –1 is returned.

The **time()** function can be called either with a null pointer or with a pointer to a variable of type **time_t**. If the latter is used, then the argument will also be assigned the calendar time.

Related functions are **localtime()**, **gmtime()**, **strftime()**, and **ctime()**.

Dynamic Allocation

There are two primary ways in which a C program can store information in the main memory of the computer. The first uses *global* and *local* variables—including arrays and structures. In the case of global and static local variables, the storage is fixed throughout the runtime of your program. For dynamic local variables, storage is allocated from the stack space of the computer. Although these variables are efficiently implemented in C, they require the programmer to know, in advance, the amount of storage needed for every situation.

The second way information can be stored is through the use of C's dynamic allocation system. In this method, storage for information is allocated from free memory as it is needed. Traditionally, the free memory region lies between your program and its permanent storage area, and the stack. In the 8086 family of processors, the location of the heap depends upon what memory model is used.

At the core of C's dynamic allocation system are the functions malloc() and free(); they are part of the standard C library. Each time a malloc() memory request is made, a portion of the remaining free memory is allocated. Each time a free() memory release call is made, memory is returned to the system. The most common way to implement malloc() and free() is to organize the free memory into a linked list. However, the ANSI C standard explicitly states that the memory management method is implementation dependent. The prototypes for the dynamic allocation functions are in STDLIB.H. The ANSI C standard specifies that the dynamic allocation system returns void pointers, which are *generic* (they may point to any object). However, some older compilers will return a char pointer. In this case, you must use an explicit type cast when assigning malloc()'s return value to pointers of other types.

The ANSI C standard defines only four functions for the dynamic allocation system: calloc(), malloc(), free(), and realloc(). However, if your computer uses a processor from the 8086 family, then your compiler will almost certainly contain several variants on these functions to accommodate the segmented memory used by these processors. If this is the case, refer to your compiler user manual.

calloc

```
#include "stdlib.h"
void *calloc(size_t num, size_t size);
```

The calloc() function allocates memory of size *num* * *size*. That is, calloc() allocates sufficient memory for an array of *num* objects of size *size*.

The calloc() function returns a pointer to the first byte of the allocated region. If there is not enough memory to satisfy the request, a null pointer is returned. It is always important to verify that the return value is not a null pointer before attempting to use it.

Related functions are free(), malloc(), and realloc().

free

```
#include "stdlib.h"
void free(void *);
```

The free() function returns the memory pointed to by *ptr* to the heap. This makes the memory available for future allocation.

It is imperative that free() only be called with a pointer
that was previously allocated using one of the dynamic
allocation system's functions (either malloc() or calloc()).
Using an invalid pointer in the call most likely will destroy
the memory management mechanism and cause a system
crash.

Related functions are calloc(), malloc(), and realloc().

malloc

```
#include "stdlib.h"
void *malloc(size_t size);
```

The malloc() function returns a pointer to the first byte of
a region of memory of size *size* that has been allocated
from the heap. If there is insufficient memory in the heap to
satisfy the request, malloc() returns a null pointer. It is
always important to verify that the return value is not a null
pointer before attempting to use it. Attempting to use a
null pointer will usually result in a system crash.

Related functions are free(), realloc(), and calloc().

realloc

```
#include "stdlib.h"
void *realloc(void *ptr, size_t size);
```

The realloc() function changes the size of the previously
allocated memory pointed to by *ptr* to that specified by
size. The value of *size* may be greater or less than the
original. A pointer to the memory block is returned because
it may be necessary for realloc() to move the block in

order to increase its size. If this occurs, the contents of the old block are copied into the new block, and no information is lost.

If *ptr* is null, then realloc() simply allocates *size* bytes of memory and returns a pointer to it. If *size* is 0, the memory pointed to by *ptr* is freed.

If there is not enough free memory in the heap to allocate *size* bytes, then a null pointer is returned and the original block is left unchanged.

Related functions are free(), malloc(), and calloc().

Miscellaneous Functions

The functions discussed in this chapter are all of the ANSI standard functions that don't easily fit in any other category. They include various conversion, variable-length argument processing, sorting, and other functions.

Many of the functions covered here require the use of the header STDLIB.H. In this header are defined the types **div_t** and **ldiv_t**, which are the types of the values returned by **div()** and **ldiv()**, respectively. Also defined is the type **size_t**, which is the unsigned value returned by **sizeof**. These macros are also defined:

Macro	Meaning
NULL	A null pointer
RAND_MAX	The maximum value that can be returned by the **rand()** function
EXIT_FAILURE	The value returned to calling process if program termination is unsuccessful
EXIT_SUCCESS	The value returned to calling process if program termination is successful

If a function requires a header file other than STDLIB.H, that will be discussed under the function description.

abort

```
#include "stdlib.h"
void abort(void);
```

The **abort()** function causes immediate abnormal termination of a program. Generally, no files are flushed. In environments that support it, **abort()** will return an implementation-defined value to the calling process (usually the operating system) that indicates failure.

Related functions are **exit()** and **atexit()**.

abs

```
#include "stdlib.h"
int abs(int num);
```

The **abs()** function returns the absolute value of the integer *num*.

A related function is **labs()**.

assert

```
#include "assert.h"
void assert(int exp);
```

The **assert()** macro, defined in its header ASSERT.H, writes error information to **stderr** and then aborts program execution if the expression *exp* evaluates to 0. Otherwise, **assert()** does nothing. Although the exact output is implementation-defined, many compilers use a message similar to this:

Assertion failed: *<expression>*, file *<file>*, line *<linenum>*

The assert() macro is generally used to help verify that a program is operating correctly, with the expression evaluating to true only when no errors have taken place.

It is not necessary to remove the assert() statements from the source code once a program is debugged. If the macro NDEBUG is defined (as anything), then the assert() macros will be ignored.

A related function is abort().

atexit

```
#include "stdlib.h"
int atexit(void (*func)(void));
```

The atexit() function causes the function pointed to by *func* to be called upon normal program termination. That is, at the end of a program run, the specified function will be called.

The atexit() function returns 0 if the function is successfully registered as a termination function, and non-zero otherwise.

The ANSI standard specifies that at least 32 termination functions may be established and that they will be called in the reverse order of their establishment.

Related functions are exit() and abort().

atof

```
#include "stdlib.h"
double atof(const char *str);
```

The **atof()** function converts the string pointed to by *str* into a **double** value. The string must contain a valid floating-point number. If this is not the case, the returned value is undefined.

The number may be terminated by any character that cannot be part of a valid floating-point number. This includes white-space characters, punctuation (other than periods), and characters other than "E" or "e". This means that if **atof()** is called with "100.00HELLO", the value 100.00 will be returned.

Related functions are **atoi()** and **atol()**.

atoi

```
#include "stdlib.h"
int atoi(const char *str);
```

The **atoi()** function converts the string pointed to by *str* into an **int** value. The string must contain a valid integer number. If this is not the case, the returned value is undefined; however, most implementations will return 0.

The number may be terminated by any character that cannot be part of an integer number. This includes white-space characters, punctuation, and characters other than "E" or "e". This means that if **atoi()** is called with "123.23", the integer value 123 will be returned and the 0.23 ignored.

Related functions are **atof()** and **atol()**.

atol

```
#include "stdlib.h"
long atol(const char *str);
```

The atol() function converts the string pointed to by *str* into a long value. The string must contain a valid long integer number. If this is not the case, the returned value is undefined; however, most implementations will return 0.

The number may be terminated by any character that cannot be part of an integer number. This includes white-space characters, punctuation, and characters other than "E" or "e". This means that if atol() is called with "123.23", the value 123 will be returned and the 0.23 ignored.

Related functions are atof() and atoi().

bsearch

```
#include "stdlib.h"
void *bsearch(const void *key, const void
              *buf, size_t num, size_t size,
              int (*compare)(const void *,
              const void *));
```

The bsearch() function performs a binary search on the sorted array pointed to by *buf* and returns a pointer to the first member that matches the key pointed to by *key*. The number of elements in the array is specified by *num* and the size of each element (in bytes) is described by *size*.

The function pointed to by *compare* is used to compare an element of the array with the key. The form of the *compare* function must be as follows:

```
int func_name (const void *arg1, const *arg2);
```

It must return values as described in the following table.

Comparison	Value Returned
arg1 is less than *arg2*	Less than 0
arg1 is equal to *arg2*	0
arg1 is greater than *arg2*	Greater than 0

The array must be sorted in ascending order, with the lowest address containing the lowest element.

If the array does not contain the key, then a null pointer is returned.

A related function is qsort().

div

```
#include "stdlib.h"
div_t div(int numerator, int denominator);
```

The div() function returns the quotient and the remainder of the operation *numerator/denominator* in a structure of type div_t.

The structure type div_t is defined in STDLIB.H and will have at least these two fields:

```
int quot;  /* the quotient */

int rem;   /* the remainder */
```

A related function is **ldiv()**.

exit

```
#include "stdlib.h"
void exit(int exit_code);
```

The **exit()** function causes immediate, normal termination of a program.

The value of *exit_code* is passed to the calling process, usually the operating system, if the environment supports it. By convention, if the value of *status* is 0 — or **EXIT_SUCCESS** — normal program termination is assumed. A non-zero value or **EXIT_FAILURE** is used to indicate an implementation-defined error.

Related functions are **atexit()** and **abort()**.

getenv

```
#include "stdlib.h"
char *getenv(const char *name);
```

The **getenv()** function returns a pointer to environmental information associated with the string pointed to by *name* in the implementation-defined environmental information table. The string returned must never be changed by the program.

The environment of a program may include such things as path names and devices online. The exact nature of this data is implementation-defined. You will need to refer to your compiler's user manual for details.

If a call is made to **getenv()** with an argument that does not match any of the environment data, a null pointer is returned.

A related function is **system()**.

itoa

```
#include "stdlib.h"
char *itoa(int num, const char *str, int
            radix);
```

The **itoa()** function is not currently defined by the ANSI standard, but it is found with many compilers.

The **itoa()** function converts the integer *num* into its string equivalent and places the result in the string pointed to by *str*. The base of the output string is determined by *radix*, which, generally, may be in the range 2 through 16.

The **itoa()** function returns a pointer to *str*. Usually, there is no error return value. Be sure to call **itoa()** with a string of sufficient length to hold the converted result.

Related functions are **atoi()** and **sscanf()**.

labs

```
#include "stdlib.h"
long labs(long num);
```

The **labs()** function returns the absolute value of *num*.

A related function is **abs()**.

ldiv

```
#include "stdlib.h"
ldiv_t ldiv(long numerator, long
             denominator);
```

The ldiv() function returns the quotient and the remainder of the operation *numerator/denominator*.

The structure type ldiv_t is defined in STDLIB.H and will have at least these two fields:

long quot; /* the quotient */

long rem;   /* the remainder */

A related function is div().

longjmp

```
#include "setjmp.h"
void longjmp(jmp_buf envbuf, int status);
```

The longjmp() function causes program execution to resume at the point of the last call to setjmp(). These two functions are C's way of providing for a jump between functions. Note that the header SETJUMP.H is required.

The longjmp() function operates by resetting the stack to the state described in *envbuf*, which must have been set by a prior call to setjmp(). This causes program execution to resume at the statement following the setjmp() invocation. That is, the computer is "tricked" into thinking that it never left the function that called setjmp(). In effect, longjmp() sort of "warps" across time and (memory)

space to a previous point in your program without having
to perform the normal function return process.

The buffer *evnbuf* is of type `jmp_buf`, which is defined in
the header SETJMP.H. The buffer must have been set
through a call to `setjmp()` prior to the calling of `longjmp()`.

The value of *status* becomes the return value of `setjump()`
and may be interrogated to determine where the long jump
came from. The only value not allowed is 0.

It is important to understand that the `longjmp()` function
must be called before the function that called `setjmp()`
returns. If not, the result is technically undefined. (Actually,
a crash will almost certainly occur.)

By far the most common use of `longjmp()` is to return from
a deeply nested set of routines when an error occurs.

A related function is `setjmp()`.

ltoa

```
#include "stdlib.h"
char *ltoa(int long num, const char *str,
           int radix);
```

The `ltoa()` function is not currently defined by the ANSI
standard, but it is found in many C compilers.

The `ltoa()` function converts the `long` integer *num* into its
string equivalent and places the result in the string pointed
to by *str*. The base of the output string is determined by
radix, which, generally, may be in the range 2 through 16.

The **ltoa()** function returns a pointer to *str*. Usually, there is no error return value. Be sure to call **ltoa()** with a string of sufficient length to hold the converted result.

Related functions are **itoa()** and **sscanf()**.

qsort

```
#include "stdlib.h"
void qsort(void *buf, size_t num, size_t
           size, int (*compare)
           (const void *, const void *));
```

The **qsort()** function sorts the array pointed to by *buf* using a quicksort. The quicksort is generally considered the best general-purpose sorting algorithm. Upon termination, the array will be sorted. The number of elements in the array is specified by *num* and the size of each element (in bytes) is described by *size*.

The function pointed to by *compare* is used to compare an element of the array with the key. The form of the *compare* function must be as follows:

int *func_name* (const void **arg1*, const void **arg2*);

It must return values as described here:

Comparison	Value Returned
arg1 is less than *arg2*	Less than 0
arg1 is equal to *arg2*	0
arg1 is greater than *arg2*	Greater than 0

The array is sorted in ascending order, with the lowest address containing the lowest element.

A related function is bsearch().

raise

```
#include "signal.h"
int raise(int signal);
```

The raise() function sends the signal specified by *signal* to the executing program. It returns 0 if successful, non-zero otherwise. It uses the header file SIGNAL.H.

A related function is signal().

rand

```
#include "stdlib.h"
int rand(void);
```

The rand() function generates a sequence of pseudo-random numbers. Each time it is called, an integer between 0 and RAND_MAX is returned.

A related function is srand().

setjmp

```
#include "setjmp.h"
int setjmp(jmp_buf envbuf);
```

The setjmp() function saves the contents of the system stack in the buffer *envbuf* for later use by longjmp(). It uses the header file STDJMP.H.

The setjmp() function returns 0 upon invocation. However, longjmp() passes an argument to setjmp() when it executes, and it is this value (always non-zero) that will appear to be setjmp()'s value after a call to longjmp().

See the longjmp() description for additional information.

A related function is longjmp().

signal

```
#include "signal.h"
void (*signal(int signal, void
              (*func)(int))) (int);
```

The signal() function defines the function *func* to be executed if the specified signal *signal* is received. The operation of this function is somewhat implementation-specific. The following discussion will give you a rough idea of its operation.

The value of *func* may be one of the following macros, defined in SIGNAL.H, or the address of a function.

Macro	Meaning
SIG_DFL	Use default signal handling
SIG_IGN	Ignore the signal

If a function address is used, the specified function will be executed.

A related function is raise().

srand

```
#include "stdlib.h"
void srand(unsigned seed);
```

The srand() function is used to set a starting point for the sequence generated by rand(). (The rand() function returns pseudo-random numbers.)

The function srand() is generally used to allow multiple program runs using different sequences of pseudo-random numbers by specifying different starting points. However, you can generate the same pseudo-random sequence over and over again by calling srand() with the same seed each time before starting the sequence.

A related function is rand().

strtod

```
#include "stdlib.h"
double strtod(const char *start, char **end);
```

The strtod() function converts the string representation of a number stored in the string pointed to by *start* into a double and returns the result.

The strtod() function works as follows. First, any white-space character in the string pointed to by *start* is stripped. Next, each character that comprises the number is read. Any character that cannot be part of a floating-point number will cause this process to stop. This includes white-space characters, punctuation (other than periods), and characters other than "E" or "e". Finally, *end* is set to point to the remainder, if any, of the original string. This means that if strtod() is called with "100.00 pliers", the value 100.00 will be returned, and *end* will point to the space that precedes "pliers".

If a conversion error occurs, strtod() returns either HUGE_VAL for overflow or −HUGE_VAL for underflow. If no conversion could take place, then 0 is returned. In either case, the global variable errno is set to ERANGE, indicating a range error.

A related function is atof().

strtol

```
#include "stdlib.h"
long strtol(const char *start, char **end,
            int radix);
```

The strtol() function converts the string representation of a number stored in the string pointed to by *start* into a long and returns the result. The base of the number is determined by *radix*. If *radix* is 0, the base is determined by rules that govern constant specification. If *radix* is a value other than 0, then it must be in the range 2 through 36.

The strtol() function works as follows. First, any white-space character in the string pointed to by *start* is stripped. Next, each character that comprises the number is read. Any character that cannot be part of a long integer number will cause this process to stop. This includes white-space characters, punctuation, and characters. Finally, *end* is set to point to the remainder, if any, of the original string. This means that if strtol() is called with "100 pliers", the value 100L will be returned, and *end* will point to the space that precedes "pliers".

If a conversion error occurs, strtol() returns either LONG_MAX for overflow or LONG_MIN for underflow, and the global errno is set to ERANGE, indicating a range error. If no conversion could take place, then 0 is returned.

A related function is atol().

strtoul

```
#include "stdlib.h"
unsigned long strtoul(char *start, char
                      **end, int radix);
```

The strtoul() function converts the string representation of a number stored in the string pointed to by *start* into an unsigned long and returns the result. The base of the number is determined by *radix*. If *radix* is 0, the base is determined by rules that govern constant specification. If *radix* is specified, it must be in the range 2 through 36.

The strtoul() function works as follows. First, any white-space character in the string pointed to by *start* is stripped. Next, each character that comprises the number is read. Any character that cannot be part of an unsigned long integer number will cause this process to stop. This includes white-space characters, punctuation, and characters. Finally, *end* is set to point to the remainder, if any, of the original string. This means that if strtoul() is called with "100 pliers", the value 100L will be returned, and *end* will point to the space that precedes "pliers".

If a conversion error occurs, strtoul() returns either ULONG_MAX for overflow or ULONG_MIN for underflow, and the global variable errno is set to ERANGE, indicating a range error. If no conversion could take place, then 0 is returned.

A related function is **strtol()**.

system

```
#include "stdlib.h"
int system(const char *str);
```

The **system()** function passes the string pointed to by *str* as a command to the command processor of the operating system.

If **system()** is called with a null pointer, it will return non-zero if a command processor is present and 0 otherwise. (Remember, some C code will be executed in dedicated systems that do not have operating systems and command processors.) The ANSI standard states that the return value of **system()**, when called with a pointer to a command string, is implementation-defined. However, generally it will return 0 if the command was successfully executed, non-zero otherwise.

A related function is **exit()**.

va_arg, va_start, and va_end

```
#include "stdarg.h"
type va_arg(va_list argptr, type);
void va_start(va_list argptr, last_parm);
void va_end(va_list argptr);
```

The **va_arg()**, **va_start()**, and **va_end()** macros work together to allow a variable number of arguments to be passed to a function. The most common example of a

function that takes a variable number of arguments is
printf(). The type va_list is defined by STDARG.H.

The general procedure for creating a function that can take
a variable number of arguments is as follows. The function
must have at least one known parameter, but may have
more, prior to the variable parameter list. The right-most
known parameter is called the *last_parm*. Before any of the
variable-length parameters may be accessed, the argument
pointer *argptr* must be initialized through a call to
va_start(). After that, parameters are returned via calls to
va_arg(), with *type* being the type of the next parameter.
Finally, once all of the parameters have been read and prior
to returning from the function, a call to va_end() must be
made to ensure that the stack is properly restored. If
va_end() is not called, a program crash is very likely.

A related function is vprintf().

Index